91 Letters

Inviting Men into New Ways Of Connecting

Buddy Odom

This book of letters is dedicated to the men who call me their friend. Dentists, pastors, husbands, jokers, fathers, realtors, artists and sons. It is no small thing to call Buddy Odom your friend... for it takes great character, vision, patience, courage and forgiveness to hang in there. Because of you, I am the richest man you will ever meet.

Cover: Springvale by Kathie Odom, Oil on Linen, 16x24
KathieOdom.com

Introduction

Most of my days are spent doing one of three things. I am either traveling America as a cheerleader for my artist/wife, Kathie, writing (or preparing to write) or I am drinking coffee with a friend in my hometown of Knoxville, Tennessee.

How I relate matters to me. It illuminates who I am, what drives me, how I see people, what I believe, how I am motivated, how highly I think of myself, what is my position before God, how well am I listening or how I am connecting. Relating as God relates (within Himself as a Three-in-One God) encourages me to ask: do conversations really matter, am I bored, do I talk too much, is prayer important and is my love real?

I awoke one morning in April of 2016 and decided to write about these questions to men like me who care about their life in Christ. They too are hungry to connect in real ways with wives to whom they made vows, and with their Godly Family to whom they belong. It gained some momentum within me and I felt a great encouragement to continue.

This short book is the compilation of ninety-one weekly notes to men. While addressed to men, women may also gain a little ground as they read. Not every man is like me, thank God, but we do share a mutual DNA spirit.

To the date of this publication I am still writing weekly to men. If you would like #92 and beyond, log onto BuddyOdom.com to subscribe. If the website is no longer available, just call or text me at 865-382-2288.

In reading, may you know Him, the only true God and Jesus Christ whom He sent.

#1

Dear Men,

I awoke this morning with this on my mind.

My way of seeing has changed since leaving the Young Life staff almost twelve years ago. It is not better necessarily... just different. And it will not surprise you to know the vehicle for this change: I am a firsthand witness to the magic of Kathie's artistry.

Kathie graduated as an art major at The University of Tennessee but quickly shelved it all after college because we married. Pause here. Doesn't that sound odd? It was not Buddy Odom who shelved things "because we married"; it was Kathie. As a matter of fact, our life <u>together</u> was more like an extension of <u>my</u> life. We did not board a new journey together, she just jumped in the passenger seat of my ride.

Looking back, our life together has been shaped by two major things: 1) We raised three children. They took (and we gave them) our thoughts and efforts and time. 2) The places my vocation carried us. It was the wind of my job that blew us here and there. Yes, we sought for God's future and blessing over our decisions. Yes, it was Him ultimately carrying us. And yes, He redeemed and is redeeming ALL of it. But notice what is missing in these two shaping agents – Kathie.

Three years ago she asked me, "Honey, what did you think about marrying an artist?" A long pause and then my admission: "It never occurred to me."

My friend, watch how God redeems your neglect. Confess your neglect. And repent, for there is no Godliness without repentance. BUT, waste no emotional, mental or spiritual space within yourself with shame or guilt. He has redeemed and will redeem ALL your neglect. ALL your foolishness. ALL the things said and unsaid to your wife and children. ALL your failed financial decisions. And yes, ALL your poor judgement and filthy thoughts. ALL.

Case in point: Twelve years later, I see differently.

I could give several scriptures at this point to shape the rest of this email. Instead, I want to share a quote from a Mississippi artist that speaks to my way of "seeing" now. Marc Hanson says:

To me, there's a difference, not better or worse, between painting those things we see, very well and with excellence, and striving to express a guttural reaction to that stimulus. That is the daily struggle in my mind. Getting the T's crossed and the i's dotted just isn't enough. I'd rather paint one painting a month, a year, that says what I feel inside, than paint twenty a day that don't. One perfectly expressed painting per decade would seem prolific in that case."

When I am awakened by the Great One who lives within, is my first reaction to share it with others because it is good? Or do I dive a bit deeper into the Source of it all, the Person. And in knowing Him, the only true God and Jesus Christ whom He has sent (Jn. 17:3), may my way of seeing change from packaging my ministry to simply walking with Him while living near others?

Somehow, my neglect and foolishness is being used to bring me to this place.

To the King
BuddyO

#2

Dear Men,

Most of you received a letter (#1) from me earlier in the week.

I must have stirred something up, because I have received MANY thoughtful responses! I don't want to clog your mailbox, but from time to time I may drop another note to the group of now 70+ men receiving this, all hungry for more God.

Since Kathie was the impetus for my last letter, I thought it was a good idea to read it to her. She was glad that I wrote and sent it to you. Here is a piece of our conversation:

K - I want these guys to know one more thing.
B - What's that?
K - You remember when you mentioned your neglect of me and how we "did not board a new journey together"? Of how I just jumped in the passenger seat of *your* ride?
B - Yes, I do.
K - You know that you didn't force me, right? I willingly got into the passenger seat.
B - Sounds like both of us were neglectful of you.
K - Exactly! You can't claim all the fault or carelessness. My desire to hide behind you coupled with your neglect made for a mess.
B - A mess that is being redeemed.
K - Your email was not primarily about me or my new work as an artist, was it?
B - Right. It was about God shaping the way I see things now, mainly through my failures, especially through my years of ignoring you. It's about His redemption of the mess WE made together and the mess we ARE together. We are two redeemed souls who continue to be and make messes... with the emphasis on REDEEMED.

On this Maundy Thursday, my friends, take some time (maybe even this moment) to bow before him in confession and repentance.

Sunday is coming.

To the King,
BuddyO

#3

Dear Men,

Last time I wrote about the route God is taking me to shape my way of seeing. It is true, is it not, that the main vehicle God uses for shaping us more into the likeness of His Son is primary relationships. In my case, Kathie followed by children, parents, siblings, close friends, etc.

It is also true that books, scripture, sermons and education play a role in the shaping of my soul. But not with the same power that relating does.

- Relating is available to all regardless of intellect or literacy.
- Relating is the field for playing with new ideas introduced by sermons and school.
- And Right Relating (Jesus calls this Righteousness) is the mirror we are given to discover how deep our ugliness runs and how deeper still is the One who forgives all that ugliness.

While the theme of scripture is good news to all, it is not alive. Because it is not a person.

In step with the Person, Jesus, are the scriptures... not the other way around.
Jesus, the Person, is the One we need. (Subtly, I dared to say here that scripture is not what we need FIRST. It is the Person that we can't live without. See John 5:39-40)

Quite often now, I am noticing how much of my life I navigate without Him. I have developed (through books, scripture, a good friend's faith, sermons and education) a way of living that requires little of Him. I make decisions, wise decisions I call them, that hinge more on experience, smarts, trial/error and observations than on the need of the relationship I have been given.

But the thing I cannot escape, try as I may (and I do!), is relationships.

- When I try to avoid eye contact with my next door neighbor who irritates me, I end up more disturbed that I want to escape yet-another possible odd conversation.
- When I wait a long time to check in on my Mom, I find it difficult to sidestep the reality: What is it in me that is so bold with some but shrinks away from the hard efforts of building a deeper friendship with her?
- If I am paying attention to my interior world while having coffee with a friend, I often discover that instead of quieting my soul (especially when confused or not knowing what to say) I try to figure him out.

As obvious as the nose on my face is THE reason I try to escape or manage all the relationships I have, especially the primary ones. Because <u>my way of relating</u> shows me things about myself that are painfully difficult to stand up under.

Hmm, I need Him.
I need Him to help me stand.

When you find a person who is gaining in true wisdom and insight, you will find a person whose muscles ache from his fight to allow Jesus to hold him up. When "called out" this same person will not give you false humility, instead they 1) will hardly know what you are talking about because they are more in touch with their own spiritual disabilities. And 2) they simultaneously see both their ugliness and their power. They see that they are participants in the Divine Nature. And at moments they are even alive with it...

As they step into the relationships they have been given.

To the King,
BuddyO

#4

Dear Men,

Lately I find that I am having more and more conversations about what I have written in the last few emails. It seems that this "relating" thing is not really a thing, but the way we are wired. The way in which we relate exposes the rich and exhausting parts of me to others, especially to those primary relations where I spend so much of my ordinary moments.

I was sitting in a small group this morning where a few of you were present. Randy (that's not his name, just my favorite alias) spoke about how difficult church has been for him. Another then asked, "Hey Buddy, when Randy was talking about his church frustrations, what was happening in you?"

My answer (and what I am about to write about) has been at the core of my recurring chats with folks over the last couple of weeks... some of my expanded thoughts on following the Affectual Track.

Connecting with others awakens me. Sitting in a structured small group, catching up on the day with Kathie, drinking coffee with a friend or speaking a casual hello in the grocery are all ways where my affections (beautiful ones AND ugly ones) are most engaged. Whether anticipating the conversation or sitting in the middle of it or considering the aftermath, my affections seek to dominate my soul. Not only does my mind engage but also my emotions, my intellect, my will (strong or weak), my social style, my body and so on. But all of these capacities (and more!) are included within my SOUL which is accessed by my affections. When I show up, I show up as a Soul, a Redeemed Soul where the Great One resides. Here He both enables and forgives these affections.

For instance, while in the midst of an active relationship (conversing or listening) my mind may disagree or my emotions may get stepped on or my will might want to voice an opinion or my social-ness might want to make you feel good or I might even want to touch your arm to make you sense safety. My affections are deeply engaged, often without recognition.

So, while I listen, my affections are a good track to run on. But NOT necessarily to speak those affections.

In the last several years Christians have been promoting honesty, vulnerability, having a voice and authenticity in conversations with one another (four GREAT things!) But what seems to rule in this sort of relating is this: The presence and movement of the Holy Spirit is replaced with subtle demands (i.e. – you must SEE me!) to make me feel better.

But if I were to pay attention to my affections and (at minimum) react internally upon those, I might be more positioned to see what God is up to in your life instead of 1) allowing you (instead of the Spirit) to pull/push me or 2) force my fears and opinions upon your present reality.

Try it.
Next conversation.
Sit with someone and hush your soul long enough to wonder (internally) about your affections.

Your mind may wander off into daydreaming. What's the Affection? Boredom.
You may remember a similar story from your own experience. Affection? The desire to connect.
You may feel unheard. Affection? The desire to correct.
Your heart may be excited. Affection? A longing for intimacy.

Then wonder, do I put voice to this? You may:
1. offer an opinion (that often does not lead to deeper connection) or
2. wonder internally why this affection is present or
3. both!

At different points, you may have multiple opportunities to offer the alive affection within yourself. Remember, it may or may not be timely to share it.

Well, there might be more stories to share about all this. Instead I will practice my Affectual Track now as I sign off. Already I am aware that I will wonder what you think of me writing these words.

What is your affection? Do you want to make me feel good about writing it?

To the King,
Buddy O

#5

Dear Men,

The reason you friends are receiving these letters is very, very simple: There is a deep sense of "Write, Buddy!" within me.

So I do.
And, apart from Kathie, you are part of the 100(ish) men who are reading these.
Also, someone asked if he could share these to friends (male and female). And, for the record, I am perfectly fine with that.

This morning I am drawn to write about two closely-related narratives that I live by. These two themes make great sense to me... so that is why I live by them. BUT, I also believe that both are oh-so-subtly false and debilitating narratives.

I'm not sure where they come from and don't plan on spending any time researching, mainly because: By God and His allowing me to live these ways, He has brought me to where I am. He is patiently carrying me through my mistakes, choices and failures. And I stand (still failing) grateful that He is transforming me into the likeness of His Son and transporting me to the Kingdom (and the Kingdom to me) where we will all be like Him.

All that being said, here are those two narratives.

- There are environments that help me relate more truly to who God has made me to be.
- And there are environments that bring out the ungodliness in my ways of relating.

From the outset may I say that, in and of themselves, these narratives are NOT bad. As a matter of fact, there will come an Eternal Day when all time and space is first and there will be no more second. It is fantastic, desirable and even worth my prayers to have spacious safe settings from which to live and relate! And it is also smart and worthy to avoid and "pray away" places that awaken my ugliness to God and others.

But the combo of these two narratives have resulted in a Buddy Odom who demands.

Now, too often, I think that -
- I must have both inner and outer peace to relate well.
- A spacious calendar is needed to help me "be" with others well.
- Predictability, regularity and consistency are necessary for my wellness.
- Being seen/known allows me to enter well into a relationship.
- If I know less people, then I will be bothered less... thus leading to a well-rounded me.

(notice how often these wonderful things can be about MY wellness)
- Being misunderstood needs to be confronted so I can continue to have impact.
- Surprise is not good, or better said, I am not at my best relationally when I am caught off guard.
- Trouble alters my relational flow too.
- Busyness must be curtailed so I can be available.
- Avoid irritation and people who irritate me.
- High expectations of me need somehow to be discounted so I can stay on my spiritual course.
- Silence is required.

Wow.
All really great things! But each and every one can be a demand with which I relationally manipulate.

I have an almost 70-year-old friend who has never (apart from emergencies) prepared a meal for himself. Each meal has been cooked for him by someone... he has rarely (if ever) thought about the preparation or clean-up of a meal. A wonderful thing (eating) that his mother began, ended up being passed on as a demand or entitlement that he now requires his wife to fulfill. A good thing gone south. Debilitating. And the results of an unobserved life.

While I still like and even long for these good places, I can end up avoiding people God has given me and also never confronting my inner instincts to be in control.

May I live openly toward ALL settings and ALL people that cross my path today.
And may all good things take a back seat to the Great One's hopes for me.

To the King,
BuddyO

#6

Dear Men,

In #4, I wrote the following which has elicited some thoughts/responses/questions:

"In the last several years Christians have been promoting honesty, vulnerability, having a voice and authenticity in conversations with one another (four GREAT things!) But what seems to rule in this sort of relating is this: The presence and movement of the Holy Spirit is replaced with subtle demands (i.e. – you must SEE me!) to make me feel better."

I want to speak to this honesty thing a bit. Relationally, a lot of damage has been done lately in the name of forth-coming. Friends, pastors and therapists have championed the idea that there is beauty in pure honesty and openness. Thinking that the alternative (withholding, hiding and avoidance) is our only option, we follow their advice. Some of us tell our spouse about our sexual thought-life. In hopes of healing, we speak with primary relationships about long-ago past hurts. And we speak openly to others about a myriad of festering wounds in the name of being on the same page or "making every effort to keep the unity of the Spirit through the bond of peace" (Ephesians 4:3)

Make no mistake, I am one who supports and promotes authenticity in all relationships. But the problem lies in what the end hope is. Spilling the beans has the highest hope of healing, while thoughtful and reflective consideration has the highest hope of knowing God... which is the road to unity in the Spirit through the bond of peace.

While the vast majority of artists completely cover their canvas, Kathie is always begging her workshop students, "There is light below... let the canvas work for you!" She is not advocating a trite exposure or uncovering of the canvas for the sake of looking good, she is suggesting that there is something underneath (linen canvas) that has a texture that can be used for the sake of luminosity.

Kathie lays on a brown-ish oil paint and then strategically (although it appears random) scrapes the canvas with an old credit card. The tiny ridges in the once covered canvas are now allowed to show through, creating background and depth to the story she wishes to communicate. It is no longer two-dimensional!

What if I used the real and honest truth that exists beneath what you see in me to form and inform the ways in which I relate with you? What if I take every part of me that is alive... my desires, hurts, past, hopes, failures, schemes, successes, dreams, manipulative ways, truth-telling, hiding, etc... and allow these realities to "work for me" in my ways toward you?

Let's neither guilt ourselves to the point of deleting this short list nor abuse our relationships by dumping them on one another. Let us remember that the Light beneath is True and is a double-edged sword active, like ice-sculpting, to shape us into His Divine likeness.

To the King,
BuddyO

#7

Dear Men,

I went to bed last night quite grateful, which is new for me. Since I have such a propensity for assholeness, this thankfulness took me by surprise. You see, I had a full day of being with men (some of you) who long to relate with the energy of God.

It began with a circle of seven incredibly potent men. These men live almost covertly, quietly seasoning the culture of their community with their desire for the Person of Jesus to be known. Then I had lunch with a guy who spoke of his hope to relate more deeply (not necessarily "be on the same page") with his wife.

Relating with the energy of God... what is that? How does it happen?

Most often I relate with the energy of *me*, which is the greatest definition of assholeness. I am curved in on myself... "Incurvates in se" as Augustine coined. I live with me as the center of the universe. Now, on one hand, this is Basic Discipleship 101. But the repetitive, subtly disguised ways of selfishness run their roots deep into my relating soil, encouraging me to gloss over this saturating sin. And when I spend time considering the enormity of my *Incurvates in se*, my hopelessness fertilizes the situation. In other words, the more I realize how poor I relate with Kathie, then the more I feel my universe is threatened, then the more I fortify myself with bad relating such as retreating or excusing or justifying.

Relating with the energy of God has <u>the knowing of the Person of Jesus</u> at the center of my universe. He swallowed my sin and is underneath all of my sin. As I curve in on myself, He sits there welcoming me as His Beloved Son! He empowers me and leads me "from place to place in one perpetual victory parade!" (2 Corinthians 2:14). And these places that He leads me in are the interior places of demands, selfishness and entitlements.

Relating from this forgiven and holy-inhabited place is relating with the energy of God.
How does it happen?

Well, I'm not completely sure.
But I do know one place to begin:
Honesty through Art.

Now, stay with me just a few more sentences. Last time I wrote about how we are abusing (by demanding) honesty and vulnerability in relationships. But there is one place where brutal honesty is required... in your and my relationship with God. And the Wisdom Books lead the way (Job, Proverbs, Ecclesiastes, Song of Solomon, and the Psalms). They are first and foremost personal books of art written to God, especially the Psalms. Honesty in writing is the goal of the Psalmists.

May I invite you into the honest art of creating (Is that not what our Triune God did in the beginning?)

As you consider how to cultivate a Trinitarian way of relating this summer, maybe you consider genuine journaling or sketching or whittling or buying a harmonica.

Who knows where your stories, drawings, toothpicks or tunes might lead?

To the King,
BuddyO

#8

Dear Men,

Many times, regarding marriage, I have been asked by sincere and meaningful men, "Help me... how am I to be the Spiritual leader of my wife?"

I love how kind and hopeful a question this is. And I believe the origin of this desire is indeed of God from the core of each man and woman. Yet, as this question evolves from the core where the Divine lives, it gets stained and twisted and rearranged. It begins as, "I want to know you, God. And I want to love my wife more deeply because You love me." It ends as, "How can I arrange for my marriage to work better?"

This is not too far of a stretch for me to say because we are made in the image of the Trinity who is a Relationship. And we work out our salvation through the most tangible ways, which are primary relationships. In this case, with our spouse.

Since "arranging for a better marriage" sounds much too selfish (because it is), it gets dressed up with Spiritual talk which comes quite naturally for many of us: *Help me... how am I to be the Spiritual leader of my wife?*

When I answer this question, I try to remember that this man has God as his core. As strong as sin is in every believer, it no longer rules as his/her core passion. Remembering that, my short answer is this: *Follow your wife.*

My longer answer is: *The deeper you dig into how you relate with your wife, the more you will find out how skewed your idea of "leadership" is. When you begin to see how poorly you lead, you grow in your ability to receive God's forgiveness, opening a way for greater humility and dependence on God for relating which brings Him honor.*

We think that leadership is about a) moving forward toward God and things of God and b) creating an attractive and irresistible path of Godliness in which others may follow. But a true follower of God (not someone who believes supremely in Godly principles and righteousness) is drawn to a friend who recognizes his own personal deficiencies in their own style of relating while longing to know God first and foremost.

If you believe that this might be you (I believe it _is_ you because of Who reigns at your center), then tune in next time for the unpacking of the short answer: *Follow your wife.*

To the King,
BuddyO

#9

Dear Men,

How can one lead and follow at the same time?
What am I asking you to consider by stating: "Lead your wife by following her"?

First, let me say that I have never had more dialogue on any other topic than being a Godly husband... ever. We make vows with a woman (something you and I do not take lightly because we have been seized by God's love). And then (it surprises us how quickly) we break those vows. THEN, through embarrassment or guilt and fear, we do not talk to her about how poorly we relate... because we think it will show her what a failure, fool or terrified man I am.

Thus, I sabotage the chance at leading well in my marriage. As soon as the pastor said, *You may kiss your wife*, I began to screw up the opportunity to lead her into this new journey called marriage. And continue to screw it up over and over.

(At this point, you may be saying: "Ah come on, Buddy! Lighten up. My marriage is going well. My wife says I'm a good husband and father. I work hard to have date nights. When we fight, we work hard to stay on the same page. You're such an Eeyore! We may not be the Christian couple of the year, but we are better off than 90% of the couples I know!")

All I can say to that is this: God does not call us to relativity, He calls us to holiness. And we fall way, way short of the beauty of His plan.

But. Here is the hope.
There is a fire deep within each of us to relate with the loving power of God to the one we made vows with. However dimly, this fire exists because He knows us and we know Him, the one who forgives my failing, foolish and fearful ways over and over and over. It is this love, wrapped in unending and undeserved forgiveness, that keeps me hanging on.

The first movement of leading by following your wife is _turning toward her_. (read this sentence again).

Maybe I should stop right here and allow you to wonder... what does turning toward my wife look like? How am I presently turning away from her? Is she aware of how deeply my fears run and how I avoid more disappointment? Does she know that ways in which I treat her more like a child than a woman? Does she know how fragile I can sometimes think her to be? Does she know how I have created a persona that enables me to be in control? And how "in touch" am I with the barter system I/we have put in place for living our lives together?

All these are ways of _turning away_. But, the first movement of following your wife is _turning toward her_. Please note how "forgiveness" is at the root of this movement. Forgiving yourself as you have been forgiven. Yes, you and I do so many things (if not everything!) poorly. Not only are we forgiven of our turning away, but our turning away is redeemed! Our foolishness is His fodder!

Yep, there are two more movements that I will save for later letters.

But for now, is it possible not to shelve this one? Is it possible you could read this to your wife? Is it possible for you to also not over-analyze this, but instead see where a conversation could lead? For some of you, you may feel like it's too late. But in the Person of Christ, is anything ever too late?

When you speak to this woman with whom you made vows, be aware of this: She could respond in many ways. She may save you or excuse you (making you feel small). She may slay or accuse you (making you want to turn FURTHER away or fight back). She may thank you. She may say nothing. She may be confused, scared, hurt or elated. Or she may not even want to talk about it.

But you just turned toward her, the first movement of following her.

To the King,
BuddyO

#10

Dear Men,

If you have been following along as of late, the subject has been *leading your wife*. I have suggested that you lead by following her. And the first movement of this is: Turn toward her.

Just for the record, if I were speaking to wives I would say that the same movement applies for her… in other words, it is just as imperative that she turn toward you. Since the alter she began to fail and be foolish as well. But I am not writing to her. I am writing to you and other men who find it easier to instruct than reflect.

After reading #8 and #9 you may –

- Feel stuck or handcuffed. There are patterns of relating with your spouse that are so imbedded in your day-to-day that it seems unrealistic that anything different and good could ever arise.
- Be tempted to keep score, especially now that you've heard me say that she should turn toward me in like manner.
- Want to use this material as a means of conversation with other couples (by all means, do so) but not without allowing it to sink into your own marriage.
- Take all this with a grain of salt.
- Be overcome with a deeper sadness than you have seen in a long time.

In any case, seek to open yourself to receive the next movement.

There has never been another Kathie Odom. Ever. Kathie brings a uniqueness to the table of temperament, gifts, habits, looks, relating style, repetitive foolishness, views about church, motherliness, and fears that are shaped by her neighborhood, friends, husband, country, restaurants, calendar, vacations, kids, requests and a vast multitude of cultural factors.

But she is like all other women ever created in this... she shows the character of God as a woman.* I don't, but she does. What a wonder that she can gender-specifically and Kathie-specifically reflect the character of God that I have no way of reflecting or knowing myself without her. What a fantastic reason for me to pursue Movement #1 by turning toward her!

The second movement of leading by following your wife is: *While remembering that she belongs to Another (the King), <u>gently but surely move into her</u>.*

(read this sentence again).

I want to end with an assignment and then unpack it a bit next time.

With your imagination practice this exercise: From a side vantage point, see the two of you facing one another. Allow yourself to (still in your reverent imagination) slowly move toward her, and melt her. Spend some time now with this exercise. Take note of any and all sensations, thoughts, stories or images that come to you, no matter how normal or strange.

Until next time when we talk more about Movement#2 and
To the King,
BuddyO

* I highly recommend Larry Crabb's book, *Fully Alive* if you'd like to dig further into the ways men and women are uniquely crafted to reflect the character of God by the ways in which they relate. But I recommend nothing if it is an opportunity to intellectually escape the hard work that God is inviting you into within your own marriage.

#11

Dear Men,

I am staying in your mailbox for a good reason: May these letters irritate, encourage, provoke, dissuade, bolster, haunt or enable you to relate like God relates. But more than anything, may they do something to allow you to know Him, the only true God and Jesus Christ whom He has sent. (Jn.17:3)

By review, I began #8 with the suggestion that we commonly lead our spouse toward God by walking as an example for her to follow... much like hiking single file on a mountain trail, Buddy in the front and Kathie behind me. I propose that we follow her instead, and in #9 and #10, I began to unpack what that means by way of *movements*.

Movement #1 addresses a paradigm shift - *Turn Toward Her*. It sounds simple but, if you are like me, you know how difficult this movement is, how difficult turning toward her CAN be and how difficult it WILL be. But all things shift when God enables me to do what I did at the alter by facing her, seeing her, and loving her again with a first love.

(May I stop here to underscore this: I can do nothing on my own. I often wonder if there is even such a thing in me called *willpower*. On my own I can do nothing good at all, but as a Christian He-in-me does good, good work. Meanwhile, in all practicality it feels more like a dance... a Divine dance where I do not disappear within Him nor He in me! Someday we will all know this mystery in entirety, but now only dimly. May this sometimes-fluid-but-mostly-stumbling-dance-with-God cause me to lean increasingly upon Him, the Great Partner).

Movement #2 - *Move Into Her*. With an exercise I invited you to pay attention to how you felt about living inside of her. (It may feel strange to stretch our imaginations like this, but we're all grownups here, yes?). I hope you spent some time noting your sensations...

what did you notice about her when you did that? What did you notice of yourself? Were you fearful or hopeful as you approached "moving in"? Did you see her as weak and overpowered by your advance or see her as strong and present? Once you were within her, did you resist looking around or stand tall?

You and I have attended enough marriage ceremonies to hear how an other-centered marriage is to be. We hear of Jesus as the groom of His church (us) the bride, and long for our own relationships to mirror this intimacy that Christ gives us. He created us with an intrinsic knowledge that, as my friend Jim McKinney is fond of saying, "The nature of the universe is giving, not getting".

The number one desire I hear from folks looking for a home-church, a people of God to live some life with, is this: Where can I be known? But the problem with that desire is now obvious... it is so me-centered. It is about getting, not giving. Being known, not knowing. Who will love me, not who may I love.

In closing, may I suggest that you and I marinate in this prior paragraph? Allow yourself to sit in two realities... 1) Yes, I find it near impossible to move into my wife, or any other relationship, because I make it about me. I demand to be known and loved instead of knowing and loving all those God puts in front of me on a daily basis. 2) As one who is already known and loved by God, I have a new center, a Center that desires to love back more than receive, to give instead of get.

God, again my sin wants to anchor me in a deep ocean of guilt and shame. But how true and right and sure is Your forgiveness! Patiently keep retrieving me from myself. Remind me. Enable me. Send me. To move in. Amen.

To the King,
BuddyO

#12

Dear Men,

Movement #3 - *Give Yourself.*

To lead your wife, you follow her by turning toward her, moving into her and giving yourself.

You give your failing, brilliant, insightful, foolish, extraordinary, weak, bodacious, complex, self-centered, momentarily-sweet, sometimes-raging, surprising, thoughtful, secretive, intentional, forgetful, steady, fluctuating, over-analyzing, deserving, anal-retentive, serving, entitled, profound, rarely-peaceful, engaged, aloof, fearful and FORGIVEN self to your wife. As you turn, as you move and as you give, you remember that you are this roller-coaster of a man made by God that is permanently tied to His tracks by the death and resurrection of His Son. You do things well, but more often, you do things poorly. But do not allow that fact to stop you from Movements #1-3.

Christ the Groom leads us by turning toward us, His bride, moving into us and continually giving Himself by the power of His Spirit.

Lord, may we as well, by Your Spirit, give ourselves one to another... not thinking so highly of ourselves but regarding one another as more important than our very selves. This we cannot do by teaching or by preaching, by willful choice or by disciplined living. We MUST be carried by You into this sort of leadership, whether with our spouse, our church or our vocation. Now aid us, O Lord, in our roller-coaster attempts at teaching, preaching, choosing and disciplines. May we live free and forgiven by the way we relate... a reflection of Your Very 3-Person Self. Amen.

Lord have mercy, Christ have mercy.

To the King,
BuddyO

#13

Dear Men,

After spending several letters and paragraphs on the invitation into a different sort of leadership, more questions than answers remain. "Can you unpack that more?" is a common inquiry in my follow-up conversations.

Because of my wife's vocation I spend a considerable amount of time with artists. I watch Kathie and her peers sit, look, and receive what sits in front of them before painting... internalizing and interpreting. But this whole process of receiving is slow and must occur in patient waiting. Regardless of their outward appearance, there is a vigilant interior stillness that characterizes the great artists. Thus, their art often leaves us, the viewer, with more questions for the artist such as, "How did you do that?"

I am drawn to the words of art historian, Sister Wendy Beckett: "To verbalize all this at once is to diminish its power. The need to keep silence is significant."

If there is a need within you to understand your wife more fully, to explain the difference or distance between the two of you, then keeping silence might be the order of business. To sit and simply receive this woman sitting in front of you is enough. Mystery needs to be received not analyzed.

Yes, the people of our daily world demand meaning and explanation. And so do I. My interior default system is sin-wired to ask, Why? What do I do next? How? To what end?

Like the great artists, the one who is inhabited by the Christ must learn to find comfort in the questions God brings with His presence. You and I are invited into relationships that are packed full of "Why? What do I do next? How? To what end?". But if God would aid us to keep silent in our demands to know how to navigate, then a gladness might faintly arise. And maybe, just maybe, I might stop acting like I am in control of my life.

May you know a vigilant interior stillness this day,

To the King,
BuddyO

#14

Dear Men,

Last night I reached page 100 in a novel.

Although everyone on this planet (it seems) has read this book, it is a book I know nothing about... ABSOLUTELY nothing! I have heard the title my whole life and had a copy or two on my shelves. It is my son's favorite book of all time.

But, again, I know nothing of the story.

While everyone else has a thought about the person of Atticus Finch, I have none.
While others see why it is a sin *To Kill a Mockingbird*, I do not.
And while so many have experienced the emotions that have yet to be revealed to me by reading this book, I have gone about living my life.

In my letter from last week, I stated, "Maybe I might stop acting like I am in control of my life." Soon after writing these words I had three men tell me how important that sentence was to them.

I have been so busy writing my story, living from the false narrative that it is up to me to finish well, that I have failed (I continue to fail) to embrace the fact that I am neither the main character in my life nor the simple reader of a story unfolding before me.

The circumstances of my life - the deaths of self, the pains of being alone, the lost-ness in marriage, the confusion over the process of sanctification, the questioning of parental relations, the embarrassment of my repetitive sin, the fear of tomorrow, the tension over competing views and opinions, the curiosity over my health, the long years of never truly being known by another, the angst of being found out – are not to be controlled, nor explained away with a good metaphor or used as a lesson.

While being the smartest person who has ever lived, Jesus was not just a teacher of lessons. He did not simply come to be a model for us. His existence on earth was not to give us a set of Godly guidelines from which to manage our own story.

Because of its overuse, it is risky to use this word picture. But it is so spot on...
He came (He comes) to invite us into a dance with Him.

Finish your life well, the invitation still stands.
Finish poorly, the invitation still stands.
Understand, be confused, hurt, be happy, gain insight or live in the dark...
The invitation to dance with Him still stands.

It's not about taking the reins or getting my theology in order. It's not about seeing the future or understanding the present moment that is sometimes debilitating. It is not about discovering what He is "trying to teach me".

The invitation is to dance. Like the first dance of a bride and groom at their wedding.

We are the bride.
While being led, we will dance well and we will dance poorly.
Receive His certain presence in the new and awkward ways of opening yourself to Him.

Don't just watch.
Be the writer AND the reader.
Let it come to you just like the end of a book surely comes.
And is coming to each of us even now...

To the King,
BuddyO

#15

Dear Men,

I have been invited to write for a couple of art blogs out there. Here is one I wrote addressed to a fictitious "Matt". But it was really written to you guys:

Dear Matt,

I often get so caught up in the hurry of life so much that I forget to ask about the things that matter. But after our lively conversation over drinks last week, I was reminded how good it is to simply catch up with an old friend.

You were very curious about my marriage and relationship with Kathie. As we talked, you often seemed puzzled over the amount of time and effort I invest into the pursuit of her art career. Most striking to me was your statement as you were leaving, "Well, I guess it's my wife's turn to do her thing now!"

I think I was misunderstood.

Here are some truths:
- Yes, as soon as Kathie and I married, I gladly took on the burden of financial provision for our family.
- Yes, we worked hard to find a vocation that intersected with my passions.
- Yes, I found a great measure of personal satisfaction upon finding that job.
- And yes, even while shelving her creative gifts for almost thirty-five years to raise kids and send me into my vocation, she deeply enjoyed watching me thrive!

I can see, Matt, how you might think I have allowed Kathie to now "have her turn" in this rocketing art career of hers. And I can see how it looks to watch me champion, promote and support her in every way I can think of.

But her new path was not mine to give. And this cheerleading of mine was not born out of a need for equity or fairness. Instead it began with an honest look at two things.

First, I started to look at my own ignorance. (I mean this word in the truest sense, not mean-spirited). I *ignored* several things that were perfectly within my vision to see, but mostly Kathie! I was so consumed with good things that I quickly began missing this young woman with whom I made vows. A few years ago after her career started to blossom, she asked me, "What were you thinking when you married an artist?" Frankly, I had no answer for her because I was busying myself with the pursuit of a wonderful life. You know… three kids, two cars, one house and a full belly.

Secondly, Kathie conveniently hid behind this wonderful life we had (have). But it was easier, much easier for Kathie to *not* paint. While extraordinarily demanding, it was somehow simpler to be the generous and kind woman who loved and encouraged a family while neglecting that once-fascinating and forever-stimulating joy of creating! Sure, she kept her juices flowing and hands busy with productive endeavors, but something was missing.

Make no mistake, Matt. While this life together is not completely ironed out, both Kathie and I are living with no regrets. And we know this crazy life cannot be settled with simplistic rules of fairness. Instead, we want to live vibrantly today without knowing what tomorrow holds.

The poet, Rainer Rilke, puts it this way: *I beg you, to have patience with everything unresolved in your heart and to try to love the questions themselves as if they were locked rooms or books written in a foreign language. Don't search for the answers, which could not be given to you now, because you would not be able to live them. And the point is to live everything. Live the questions now. Perhaps then, someday far in the future, you will gradually, without even noticing it, live your way into the answer.*

Clearly, there is a celebration going on over Kathie's quiet success. Her oil paintings continue to evolve as do her relationships within a vast art-loving community. She is not hiding as much and I am, thank God, not quite so blind.

And I am one proud husband that will follow her anywhere she wants to go.
But I must remember. She is a book written in a foreign language.

Man, I love this book.

To the King,
BuddyO

#16

Dear Men,

While in the mountains a couple weeks ago I saw an old, inviting cabin with a quiet place to sit in its backyard of Mountain Laurel. So alluring was the summer coolness of this spot, I decided to knock on the door to see if I could borrow the quiet for an hour or two.

Above the porch hung a small sign notifying me of the owners: Pud and Slim Wilson. As I rapped on the single-paned glass I wondered, "Which of the married couple would be Pud and which would be Slim?"

A tall 80+ year-old man with few wrinkles and piercing blue eyes answered the door with a faint smile. Slim (I didn't call him this, it was just obvious) answered my request with an openness of his own. I immediately felt at home with this mild and peaceful man and began a conversation about his life. "Oh, this is my parents old home place. Pud and I come here to the mountains once a year. I only get two weeks vacation each year because... well, I'm a Baptist preacher from South Georgia."

There was a pause.
He had no idea what I was thinking. And I had no idea what were to be his next words.

What happens in a moment like this for you? (I'll tell you what transpired between us momentarily.) But first, would you be willing to ponder what would commonly be your interior reaction to his comment? What style of relating would normally kick into gear with you? What would be the baseline of your next response?

All of our thinking has a bottom to it. All of our interior responses are driven by something. Looking deeper we can see motivations such as fear or love for another or threat or desire to make life work better or even loneliness. But underneath ALL of it there is one single driving force in each of us whether male/female, believer/non-believer, Jew/Gentile. It is this: Hunger.

Two Christian men facing one another in rich conversation.
One says, "I'm a Baptist preacher from South Georgia."
I cannot tell exactly what came alive within *him* during the pause, but one might guess after hearing him continue with these words: "I'm Independent Baptist, not Southern Baptist… there is a BIG difference!"

Slim is hungry to have a doctrine that makes sense. But at a core level, he is hungry for more of what, or may I say Who, he was made for. And, since neither Slim nor I nor you can have Jesus completely yet, we hunger – to understand, to be known, to have impact, to create, to love, to have a people, to laugh, to be at home, to be seen, to be filled, to relate like God does, to know perfect peace.

Our hunger cannot fully be met until The Day. While knowing that truth, we still relate in ways to satisfy the hunger. We explain ourselves, choose sides or doctrines, join a particular church, analyze, examine, fight, argue, split up, like or dislike, applaud or boo. All in the name of satisfying a hunger that cannot be satisfied until heaven.

While remembering that the correct answer is *I hungered,* what ran through my mind and heart during that pregnant pause?

- If I'm not careful, Slim may find out what my church background is.
- I really like this soft, strong man.
- I don't really care what the difference is between Independent and Southern Baptists.
- Damn, all I wanted was a couple hours of quiet and here I am running into another pastor!
- This conversation was delightful until it turned toward denominations.
- What are you up to God?

All these (and more) happened within me, but all of these were motivated by a hunger *to know God completely.*

I am not happy to say that my standard way of relating won. When Slim spoke of his differences I did not see him as hungry. Actually I ceased seeing him at all. I missed the opportunity to allow this man, another family member, to show me his hunger. I escaped the possibility of knowing God more fully by following his tug on my beliefs. I did not allow this beautiful child of God to shape me with his differences. A threat came and I ducked.

Do you know that Donald Trump is hungry?
When encountering people with different ways, do you find it hard to not be cynical or threatened by his/her cultural ways?

What relationships are you saddened over at this time?
In what ways are you not seeing a hunger in them? In you?
Spend some time thinking over this idea of *hunger* and see what rises.

To the King,
BuddyO

#17

Dear Men,

It is clear that, when it comes to my relating, the most forcible and shaping authority is ME. It doesn't take a rocket scientist to realize that each of us are influenced most greatly by the desire to please ourselves. Our stomachs cry out when they are not fed and the same is true of our souls. The hunger to please ME sits at the head of the table.

But there are at least two other uninvited guests at the table. One is the most shrouded and evasive and least talked about, because we fear him. He would receive the most blame for our poor styles of relating if we dared give it to him... but rarely do we. His name is Satan. His power to persuade is both subtle and colossal.

The third uninvited guest receives the most attention. Like the child who spills the milk at every meal, our Culture is singled out and blamed most by those who wish to point out **why** I relate so poorly. Example - "Look at the circumstances of your life, Buddy, your father died when you were ten and a void was created that, while God filled it with other men, forced you to seek other ways of gaining attention. Then the culture around you reinforced this need by exhorting your spotlight-hungry spirit and encouraging your poor decision-making with applause and laughter. You have become a product of your culture. It's **their** fault!"

I do not write this tongue-in-cheek. I believe this example to be true with the exception of that last sentence. While our far-reaching and sin-soaked culture is heavy with influence, it is still only one of three ungodly ways my relating takes shape.

So, while we are on the topic of ME and CULTURE (see, here I go leaving Satan out of print), I would like to seize this opportunity to point out one of the most culturally shaping influences on my life. As I do this, would you please entertain the thought that this is a dominating factor (maybe the dominating factor) that culturally shapes the way both you and I relate with God and one another.

When I was a kid, I was bullied. Not just occasionally... I was THE kid that was bullied. Maybe it started with my chubbiness or being fresh meat in school (we moved yearly because of my dad's job) or because we lived in a mobile home. However it began, **being bullied** shaped me. I began going out of my way to avoid certain boys. When cornered, I learned to fight back. (Countless are the fist fights that I seldom shrank from and rarely won. My back was forever on the gym floor with yet another kid saddling me for free punching lessons).

Unwittingly, these kids taught me to relate as they did. And I began to bully too.

Today I see it repeated in a myriad of ways. I see it when Kathie goes out of her way to avoid my critique. I see it when I am left out of a conversation or a consideration. I see it when my definition of manliness comes into question. I see it when I am blamed. I see the ways in which I strong-arm conversations or decision-making (especially when I am the oldest in the room or the father of the family). I see the ways I influence outcomes that benefit me by offering the trump card of experience (then I cloak it with: "it's just my opinion")

Layer years upon years of this sort of relating and you will find patterns emerging. Just yesterday I had some time constraints and needed Kathie to run an errand for me. I genuinely (is that possible?) did not want her to rearrange her schedule, so I asked what her plans were for the day. Because of years of bully-style-relating, she felt cornered and threatened. I could tell she didn't receive my question very well (what great insights I have at times!) and asked her what was wrong. Her reply: "I feel managed by you."

The most practiced way of bullying is through pity. We force conversations (unconsciously, most the time) toward our favor by enticing sorrow or sympathy from another. Here are some simple examples I have honed to perfection:

- I've had a hard day.
- I couldn't get back with you because my calendar was so full.
- It is difficult for me to express myself sometimes.
- I'm tired.

And here is the most used line of them all...
- I don't know how.

We do it with God too.
- If I could only get out of debt, God, I could do more for you.
- If you would just tell me what to do, God.
- How can I enter yet another conversation with her about my failure, God? It will cause her to suffer again.

And then (with time) we begin to allow others off the hook by pitying them.
- His dad did the best he could.
- Oh, it's okay that she forgot... let's do it for her. She's just shy.
- Life has been long and hard for him.

How are you a bully? Look to your primary relationships first. And do what I did... talk with your spouse or best friend. Confessionally. Ask their forgiveness. Go to some of these places with her. Seek the wisdom of one another.

And remember: While there are three major shaping influences to my relating that sit at the table... this table of the uninvited sits in the house of God. You and I are loved and owned. We are sealed and *actively* being redeemed by the Great Within.

To the King,
BuddyO

#18

Dear Men,

I am awake late into the night which is unusual for me. I love me some cold sheets and new mattress right about now. But I can't sleep. I don't mean **can't** like I am not tired. I mean **can't** like I am troubled. My friend Mike has lung cancer.

Understand this: Mike is one of the up-teen friends I have. While our wives are much closer, Mike and I have had only one or two substantial conversations in our 35 years of friendship... *maybe* one or two. Neither of us would consider one another as "close" friends. But I still can't sleep. Or maybe I don't want to.

Mike and his wife discovered this new cancer quite recently and I sort of want to stay up... like they are right now. Somewhere in a hospital room with the beeps and interruptions we are all familiar with, Mike lies awake thinking thoughts about life. About death. About all his days accumulated behind him and the hope for more to come. And I am finding that I want to somehow join him. I want to join him in the prayer for healing. I want to feel some of his troubled heart. I want to hope with him. With them.

At my deepest place where God resides, I find myself asking this exact question right now: Who am I to be, before God, for Mike?

As I meditate on this, I remember the verse about boldly approaching the throne of grace. So I look it up (just now). Here is how *The Message* translates Hebrews 4:15-16:

We don't have a priest who is out of touch with our reality. He's been through weakness and testing, experienced it all - all but the sin. So let's walk right up to Him and get what He is so ready to give. Take the mercy, accept the help.

Who am I to be, before God, for Mike?
One who receives the loving care of Jesus.

Yes, it is me who receives the help of Jesus as I converse (with Jesus) about my friend (Mike).

Imagine me talking to God about Mike... I am standing upright, without fear (because of Jesus) right before God. He invites me and longs for me to do this. I don't know exactly what to say because of both the awesomeness of Who I am speaking with and the tragedy of Mike's illness. I know that God in Christ knows all Mike's pain and is carrying Mike, but He waits and wants me to speak with Him about Mike. What do I say or (better yet) who am I to be?

While hurting for Mike and Sandy, I am to be one who personally receives the help in my own prayers.

Help to pray.
Wow.

In my weakness to pray (that seems incomparable to Mike's physical need) God still says **take My help.**

As we seek to help others with care and prayers, may we be those who are confident only in His help, not in our own.

To the King,
BuddyO

#19

Dear Men,

I have been reading up on John Donne, the English Poet (I will tell you why momentarily). He is the one who famously wrote: "Never send to know for whom the bell tolls; it tolls for thee."

Here is the brief on him:

- He lived at the turn of the 17th century.
- His dad died when he was very young.
- Donne's Family was very devoted to Roman Catholicism which got them in deep yogurt with the Anglican's, England's adopted church.
- Before the age of 25 he received a high education while spending all his inheritance on wine, women and song.
- Although he finished, Cambridge would not give him his degree for he refused to swear allegiance to the King as supreme authority over the church of England.
- He somehow got into law school and became a chief secretary to a big dog (Sir Thomas Egerton) in the "White House" of the English Monarchs.
- He fell in love Egerton's niece and secretly married her.
- which resulted in him being fired and imprisoned (the minister who secretly married them was also put in jail).
- After his prison release he lived in deep poverty while growing anti-Roman Catholic.
- He had to live off the charity of wealthy friends.
- His wife bore 12 children (two stillbirths and three of them died before the age of ten).
- She died 5 days after giving birth to #12
- when he is 44 years of age.

- Somehow he was elected to Parliament (a non-paying job)
- But connected to some folks who paid him to write anti-Catholic poetry (bizarre, huh?)
- After some inner angst he chose to swear allegiance to the

- Church of England.
- Cambridge gave him an honorary doctorate.
- He had many posts as a chaplain and eventually became the Dean at St. Paul's Cathedral in London.
- Died at 58... that's my present age.

- Early his poetry was filled with strong language against society and he wrote some quite erotic sonnets.
- After the experience of all the deaths and poverty, he chilled out and began penning much more mellow and even gloomy writings.
- As a result he gained a deep connection to God and others.
- He understood (at some core level) the intricacies of loss and dependence.

And with a deep faith, Donne wrote: "If even a clod of dirt is swept away by the ocean, all of Europe is diminished."

You and I are making eternal connections through God to one another. When one of our bodily members aches or is lost, we become diminished... we become less.

When this happens to you (and it will), do me and yourself a few favors.

- Don't spout your theology. Feel and live your theology. Allow the ache to ripple to others who are aching.
- Live in a way that activates you to your brother and sister... like our physical body is connected finger to wrist to arm. Touch them with your words or hands, even when there is a great possibility that your words or embrace will fail them. Do it anyway... the act will win.
- Live in a way that allows yourself to hurt and look weak which leads to an even deeper and MORE eternal (is that possible?) connection.

At 58 years of age I have been given (and the people I know and love have been given - and will be increasingly given) this very opportunity. An opportunity to diminish.

This, my friends, is worth considering.

To the King,
BuddyO

#20

Dear Men,

When someone finds out that I write a weekly email to approximately 100 men, they oftentimes ask: So, what do you write about?

My common response is: The thread that invariably runs through all the emails is **Right Relating**. And this **Right Relating** is shown to us by the way the Trinity relates. The Father and the Son and the Holy Spirit relate with a perfect Other-centeredness.

As many of you know I have been loved and fed by Dr. Larry Crabb. We have spent considerable time together over the last eleven years and his books have had a tremendous impact on me. His community and family have become a part of mine and Kathie's… and we thank God often for their friendships.

In 2006 Larry said to me: "Buddy, your deepest greatness is…"

Wait.
Let's press the pause button right here.
If you're good at math, you will surmise two bodacious things to this point. 1) By using only five words it is clear to see that someone (Larry, in this case) is taking a giant step with another (Me, in this case) to dare, and 2) he knew me FOR ONLY ONE YEAR when he spoke this!

Do you live this way?
Or is this way of relating relegated to certain highly educated individuals?
Do you need initials after your name to give yourself the green light to speak this way?
Or is there some level in which to arrive before leaning into another with such boldness?
Is it **wrong relating** to speak to another like this if your words are not on target?

Said another way: Is **right relating** always articulated perfectly? What keeps you and I from living in a manner that allows the deep to speak to deep?

While I still remember what Larry spoke to me (fear not, it's coming), it was actually the power of his action plus the high chance that he could be wrong or misleading that carried the most weight with me. The "deepest greatness" of all of us is what he spoke to me, but it was his kind courage and thoughtfulness that made his words lodge deeply within me, alive even a full decade later.

"Buddy, your deepest greatness is that you have the ability and capacity to move into the reality of the Trinity."

Would you mind meditating on this being your deepest greatness too? Take a moment to write his statement down and post it to your steering wheel or mirror for a few days. See what rises up within you… how does it feel to know what your deepest greatness is? What reluctance shows up within you? Is it enlivening or too vague? At this moment are these words sparking something in you or falling numb?

Your deepest greatness is that you have the ability and capacity to move into the reality of the Trinity.

Certainly, there is much more to be said and discovered in regards to "moving into the reality of the Trinity". But IF this is the deepest greatness about you and I, then maybe it is worth first considering that **I actually have a greatness**.

You do.
As do I.
And this greatness has everything to do with a Triune God.

To the King,
BuddyO

#21

Dear Men,

Upon occasion we receive compliments. What is your tendency when this occurs? Personally I have, for most of my adult life, downplayed the comment with satire or straight sarcasm. I made fun of myself. Rarely did I let the compliment stand on its own, unsoftened by some balancing act of false humility.

Understandably, upon beginning a new life in Christ, we want to clean house. As the Indwelling Spirit of God fills our lungs with fresh words and our muscles with new ways of relating, we discover a liveliness and desire to join Him by making brave new decisions about the way we live, talk and act. The braggadocios ways of old are no longer attractive. He is changing me!

But I soon end up relying on my own power... strong-willing a form of godliness versus trusting the One who dwells within. I quickly forget that He placed greatness deep within me which is His Very Self. I am a participant in the Divine Nature.

As a result, my memory of this new experience of "Indwelling" is seldom exercised. I quickly return to ways of old where I am the captain of my own ship. And I am fortified in these old ways each Sunday by friends (like me, still practicing old ways) and a well-intentioned sermon (about implementing new strategies instead of trusting). Before I can turn around, my "new" life is guilt-laden and lacking peace. All with a boat-load of effort.

I have forgotten that I have a deep greatness... A Person lives in me.

I write all this as a way of explaining the common road of a white, male, American follower-of-Jesus and the muck we are mired in. I am building a case (if you will) for the forgiveness that invites us to return to Him over and over and over and over again... without shame.

Is it possible to live this way? Without shame or guilt? Without fear that my thought-life or foolish ways will bring me some God-like karma? (You know, that well-I-deserved-to-be-punished-by-God-because-of-what-I-did thing).

As dangerous a proposition as it may be, I deeply desire to live forgiven.
That's right... **living forgiven**, at least in the culture in which I exist, is dangerous. **Getting it right** is much more acceptable and supported.
And the only way this **living forgiven** can happen?
Remembering that I have a deep greatness about myself – Him in me.

To the King,
BuddyO

#22

Dear Men,

What is important and what is central?

These are actually two questions that (like I asked) too often get grouped into one. What is central is clearly important, but all that is important cannot be central. Only one thing can be.

Here, out of my love of Buddy Odom, is where I have gotten into a mess... I have been in a lifelong stupor of thinking too highly of myself. As a result, I have repeatedly sought to overthrow the government of my own body.

What am I saying?
There was a time that Jesus took throne over my world, not circumstantially (He did that along) but interiorly. There was a moment when I stepped down from directing my life, choosing the intent for my life, owning my life. And He moved in. It was a permanent exchange that took place; what was central is no longer. But ever since then I have tried to usurp authority of the new King of Buddy Odom.

At this point I imagine that we all are in general agreement to this paragraph describing *Basics-of-Being-a-Christian 101*. But I would like to underscore the indescribable force of this new centrality, this new core. It is a He, The Person of God. Paul calls it **Christ in me**.

Easily understood is this - **Christ in me** cannot be overthrown by my own fleshly desires or foolish choices. But (a little more difficult to realize) neither can He be replaced by important things such as:

A disciplined life.
Knowledge of the Scriptures.
Dedication to family.
Being on mission.

A consistent life of prayer.
Building a Godly church.
Inner Peace.
Or finishing well.

This small sampling of coup attempts (I have made many more) were deployed by me unwittingly and, of course, without success. I am so glad.

Listen carefully to the way Paul puts this in Colossians 2:

Entering into this fullness (Christ in me) is not something you figure out or achieve. It's not a matter of being circumcised or keeping a long list of laws. No, you're already in – insiders – not through some secretive initiation rite but rather through what Christ has already gone through for you, destroying the power of sin. (The Message)

Three astonishing words.

Christ in me is central to our entire way of being.
Christ in me is the deepest greatness you and I will ever have.
Christ in me is both the fire and fuel for right-relating.
Christ in me is what I am ultimately hungry for.
Christ in me is the route to living forgiven.
Christ in me is what allows us to move into the reality of the Trinity.

As *Insiders*, let us next time explore some reality of the Trinity.

To the King,
BuddyO

#23

Dear Men,

If my deepest greatness is that I have the capacity to enter (because of Christ in me) into the reality of the Trinity, then what on earth (or heaven) is the reality of the Trinity?

The reality of the Trinity is the theme of scripture. *Elohim* is the second most commonly used Hebrew word in the Bible which is simply translated *God*, and is seen almost 3000 times in the Old Testament. This doesn't seem to be a big thing... the word *God* appearing in the Bible, right? Yet it becomes a much bigger thing when it is understood that *Elohim* is plural.

Many theologians suggest that the plural tense was offered to show the magnitude of God in His power (i.e. – not just mighty, but mighty-mighty). But, while impossible to completely understand, couldn't it profoundly speak of God as Three-Persons-in-One-God?

What is the #1 most used word for God in the OT?
6800 times *Elohim* calls Himself *Yahweh* (translated, the LORD), which literally means *present-to-act*. THIS is the (wow!) reality of the Trinity – because of His plural-ness He is present to act!

Yahweh.
God the Father Almighty (Person 1), who has highest authority, has actively engaged (*Yahweh*) by the death/resurrection of His Son (Person 2) so I may enter the Trinity through His Spirit's (Person 3) deposit of Christ in me, which is a present and active engagement (again, *Yahweh*).

Your deepest greatness is that you have the capacity to enter His relational reality. You and I belong IN this eternally written story that dates back to the beginning of time and never ends. He is inviting me more deeply into His relational happiness, to participate (celebrate) not only the Christ in me but me in Him! No sprucing-up needed!!

A.W. Tozer says, "Some of the most rapturous moments we know will be those we spend in reverent admiration of the Godhead."

And I would clarify that "reverent admiration" is not just a quiet-time meditation upon the Three Persons in One. But it is reflecting the nature of God to others by the way I relate to them like He does with me… what He calls present-to-act. What I call Trinitarian Relating. Or simply said – the reality of the Trinity is **love**.

So, if you put me and A.W. together for a moment, you get this: "Some of the most rapturous moments we will ever know is when we love one another like God has loved us!"

Dear Men, do you have somebody to love? Let's go.
To the King,
BuddyO

#24

Dear Men,

I want to write once more about the relational reality of our Trinitarian God. Then I would like (in the next letters) to return to what it looks like to enter this battle of Trinitarian Relating in our little worlds.

But first a prayer if you don't mind:
> *Elohim, You are who You are.*
> *You are Father to all – loving, caring, shepherding, disciplining.*
> *You are Jesus – mighty to save, teaching, revealing.*
> *You are the Spirit – reminding, comforting, bringing the love of Your nature to bear.*
> *Softly press in upon me this challenging Trinitarian way of living, that I may be holy formed by Your Spirit.*
> *Amen.*

I do not know how to advance very far in my faith without seeing God as a community of Three. Seeing Him only as One is, may I dare say, extraordinarily limiting. And maybe that's why we live that way… if He is limited, I can conveniently control His range of impact on my life. As Father only, I don't share my innermost world with Him because He doesn't experience me personally. As Son only, I don't share my concerns for the future with Him because He cannot watch over me. And as Spirit only, I don't share my present needs with Him because He is some sort of untouchable hovering vapor.

But as a Perfect Community He is bound by nothing… time, circumstances, location (even my interior world), relationships, any word ever uttered, nor even in the most difficult conversation in history (Matthew 26:36-46) where this Perfect Community faced One Another. Take time to stop now and listen in by reading this passage where you will even find the words - *My Father, if there is any way, get me out of this* (MSG).

It is too simple to say that Jesus was honest and transparent with His Father. And it still falls short to say that He was authentic and genuine. A more accurate description of the eternal state of Their relational style would be – They faced inward.

Always have. Always will. The Trinity always faces inward, for They have the best interests of One Another in mind. Always. Even when Jesus "plunged into agonizing sorrow". (MSG)

Since this Perfect Community of Three has always existed, Jesus not only knew, but conceived and approved of the plan to be carried out. Plus, He had a long time (eternity) to converse intimately with His Father over this most anguishing of tasks. Yet the anxiety remained:

- This sorrow is crushing my life out. (MSG)
- My soul is overwhelmed with sorrow to the point of death. (NIV)
- My soul is exceeding sorrowful, even unto death. (KJV)

When you sense that your soul is being crushed, what is your impulse? Fight? Flight?
When someone hurts you with words, what is your reply? Gouge back? Gossip?
When loneliness shadows you, how do you respond? Detachment? Downward spiral?

Oh, to have the mind of Christ! Knowing and trusting that the love of God will never release me to destruction. Believing in and relying upon the One who lets nothing slip away without redemption. Letting His guarantee take root in me. Banking on His pledge.

Oh to battle for the mind of Christ! Entering the mystery of His ways. Dying to my fantasies. Awakening to His deeper dreams within me. Attacking areas of repetitive relational sin. Placing myself in His ways. Letting His word seep into my bones. Limping in my strengths. Striding in my weaknesses. Loving the strange love of God.

Can you see that your deepest greatness is that you have the capacity to enter into the reality of the Trinity which is to have the mind of Christ? And, oh yes, it is a battle until the end.

To the King,
BuddyO

#25

Dear Men,

I want to start this letter with two bullets -

- Twelve years ago Kathie and I moved back to Knoxville from Asheville. There have been many changes... many I say. But the one that seems to be steadiest in me (and it would be real hard to shake it... even if I wanted to) is the kinship I have with John the Baptist.
- Each December, I begin thinking about the coming year. And I sort of make a resolution, a hope to live into. In thinking about this at the end of last year (2015) I allowed my absolute greatest longing to overwhelm me. It became clear to me what my end-of-year prayer would be. As a matter of fact, this very prayer (resolution/hope/whatever you want to call it) would be the same for each and every December to come! And here it is: "At the end of this coming year, Lord, I want to have loved double... twice as well."

At first thought, these two bullets don't seem to mix very well together. But I believe you would agree, it was the Baptist's absolute greatest longing also. I want to tell you - It is a prayer that invites me more deeply into the battle to relate like God relates, Trinitarianly. And, this prayer is a prayer that God answers!

Since then, my heart is increasingly striding when I think of others... when I think of you. While living freely enough to say some of the craziest things a man could ever say to another, I have simultaneously never desired to love others or actually have loved others this well. It cannot be measured, this other-centered Spirit that grows within me AND all who are in Christ. Of course (this almost goes without saying) there is no way I will ever love enough or perfectly this side of heaven. BUT this prayer is being answered. All the time spent on judging, analyzing, correcting, comparing, straightening, adjusting, controlling, condemning, explaining, smugly smiling, subtly inserting a few choice words, strategizing, honing, preparing, and anticipating is, by God's Spirit, readily being replaced (slowly but surely) with one perfect simplicity - love.

The way it seems to happen is this:

There is a lot of space within me occupied by judging, etc. (see list above). I hate this list because He lives in me. And NATURALLY I cannot remove this list to create more space for Him... I have tried, cried and relied on all sorts of means at hand. But this is a supernatural problem, not a natural one. It must be God who SUPERNATURALLY replaces the list with love! Although I try, I simply cannot.

So, the purpose of prayer, meditation, swimming-in-scripture and other disciplines?
It is not a way of getting myself into spiritual shape.
It is my way of saying, *Here I am God. I cannot but You can and will in me.*
It is my way of saying, *This is a battle... to love as You love. Grow in me that I may love as You love.*

Crudely put, I have always imagined John the Baptist to be an ass. But He was not... he was a lover. He was one who lived a uniquely disciplined life that led him to supernaturally praying, "May I decrease and may He increase."

And I pray, may we supernaturally love double today,

To the King,
BuddyO

#26

Dear Men,

Yesterday I walked behind Kathie as we neared the south rim of the Grand Canyon. It has been a dream of hers since childhood to see what all the ruckus is about... all the talk of colors and indescribable beauty. You see, as an artist, she notices light differentiations and hue contrasts in ways that most do not. Because of the nonstop rotation of the earth or the shifting of thin atmospheric layers or the changing angles that give new position to the sun, the light on subject matter is constantly refreshing itself.

As I was saying, I stayed a few feet back to witness Kathie realize a dream. As the curtain parted, she lifted both hands to her chest and, even from behind, I could see that she had stopped breathing. ***Oh my*** were her only two words. Repeated over and over. We spent the next hours slowly walking from spot to spot drinking in the subtleties of color and texture in the stone.

This canyon, those stars and her fingers were born out of relationship. All of creation is beauty born of God giving Himself to Himself. (That's a good sentence so let me say it again). All of creation is beauty born of God giving Himself to Himself.

He even bragged on Himself giving to Himself, daily saying: ***It is Good!*** Five times He said it. But there is a great question that could be missed here – Who did He say it to? Other than the presence of the water and land and animals and soil and sky, who was there to hear His long-living proclamation? It was the Two Others in relationship with Him!

I am pointing out here that the relationship, the community of Three, and the Other-centered ways of pleasurably giving from Self to Self, ***is higher than all His handiwork.*** Which must mean this: All creation, no matter how breath-stopping or mind-blowing it is, is <u>less than</u> relationships. While it pleased the Three-in-One God to create the fabulous experiences of nature and cosmos, He is very intent on stating (as He did on Day 6) that there is something **very good!** Relationships.

There is nothing more beautiful than a relationship between two people that wants to be like God as He relates. And what is more astounding is this: We can have many of those relationships!

How all this works out is why I mistakenly make **what He did and what He is doing** bigger and more important that **who He is.** How all this relating with others works out is damn-hard! It would make much more sense to just avoid people and praise Him primarily through song and nature and experience! It would be much easier to forget being overlooked by someone than turning to this someone with other-centeredness. It would be much more strategic to follow the book of church discipline than walking the difficult path of friendship with a brother who has made life-destructive decisions.

Let me say it this way: I have allowed a doctrine of love to stay in my head for so long that actually implementing that doctrine (expressing the nature of God to another) seems foreign to me. I have expended so many days and so much energy seeking the proper experience of God instead of expressing God to others.

But His highest hope for me and you is to know Him, to know **who He is**... so that He might be expressed in love to those we have been given. Whether we like them or not.

I am married to an artist, and my life is more beautiful because of it in countless ways. I don't want the growth I am experiencing through my marriage to end. But the truest beauty is found in right-relating. Damn-hard right-relating.

To the King,
BuddyO

#27

Dear Men,

Kathie and I are planted in Sedona, Arizona this week. She was invited (along with 29 other national artists) to paint the bizarrely beautiful landscape for the local art center. As most of you know, she does six (or so) of these events each year and has had great success. We get to see a lot of our country and she is alive when brush is in hand.

Sedona is known for the new age lifestyle... psychics, crystals and vortex energies exuding from certain rock formations. There is an overt effort to gain access to a better life... you know, alignment of the stars and such.

I have to admit that, while I won't get my palm read this afternoon, none of this bothers me. I am not frowning on the town for all the cosmic promotion nor am I detecting any extra satanic activity. I just see hungry people.

Increasingly I see myself that way also. When I stumble (or fall off a cliff) in my relating, it's because I hunger for more. When I notice a nagging low-level sense of loneliness, I trace its origin back to my hunger for more.

(In the midst of my writing the above, the phone rings. It is a Sedona number so, maybe I should answer it... could be about Kathie's art. It's not.)

<u>Caller</u>: *Hello Mr. Odom. This is Robin calling you back from Verde Propane. Sorry I missed your call earlier this morning. Were you needing a propane refill for your camper?*
<u>Me</u>: *Oh, thank you Robin, but I already took care of it!*
<u>Robin</u>: *I am so sorry Mr. Odom. My husband and I have had a sad thing happen and are just now getting back to our customers. Sorry we didn't get to your call this morning.*
<u>Me</u>: *Quite alright, Robin. May I be so nosey and ask, are things ok?*

Robin: *No, my son was murdered two days ago.*

Hunger everywhere.
Hunger to know God.
And because I am writing you, I am reminded of that. So I leaned in and told her I knew God personally and would talk to Him about her and her husband and her pain... that they would be sustained by Him, to know Him.

So I will sign off and do what I promised her.

Yours hungrily and to the King,
BuddyO

#28

Dear Men,

As men we have an inherent desire to think "impact". It is in my hard-wiring to want to make a difference, to leave a legacy, to impact a people or more importantly a person. I don't want to resist this until it becomes my god (i.e. – creating the kingdom of Buddy vs. expanding the Kingdom of God for His renown).

It might be good to watch how women handle "making an impact". Since it doesn't seem to dominate how they relate (they are often surprised how impactful they can be), it might be a good thing to observe how women actually make a Godly impression on others. Often women are quietly (but not necessarily covertly) changing the way church cultures think, guiding families in good directions and encouraging new ways of thinking within primary relationships.

I am fond of telling women who are married that their husband **hears everything they say...** unless that woman is bitchy. The scripture calls this **vexing.** (Proverbs 21:19 – "It is better to live in a dessert land than with a contentious and vexing woman" NASB). When Kathie says something to me, I hear it. Yes, I am threatened sometimes and I often bight, push back, or resist, but what she says HAS impact upon me because she lives a life that is not bitchy. She is making an impact for God in me!

Yesterday was a big day. We have been traveling this month and have landed for a few days in the hill country of Texas. About an hour from where we are presently staying lives Kathie's high school art teacher. She hadn't seen her in 40 years! So we made a connection through Facebook and went to see her.

Wow! To quietly sit and watch the two of them connect. Again, wow! Art was spoken of a bit, but relating (whether they knew it or not) was the main topic. How they connected in the high school art room then, how they are connecting to others now, how God is alive within each of them, how they long to matter in the lives of their children, and how the days are fleeting. It was absolutely exhilarating to see this 70-year-old woman realize what impact she made so long ago (and even presently) upon Kathie!

As a teenager it was the very life of Claudia that Kathie watched. It was a life of the love of art that first drew Kathie in, but it was more powerfully the hunger of a young woman that longed to BE impacted!

I have written much about our hunger.

Maybe the greatest impact I can make on another is just the simple out-loud-admission to myself (while in the presence of another) that both of us are hungry for God.
Let me state that again: Maybe the greatest impact I can make on another is just the simple out-loud-admission to myself (while in the presence of another) that both of us are hungry for God.

I wish you could've been there. It was holy.
Both Claudia's husband and I were mesmerized by these women dancing together with words and longings and memories and hope.

Men, we have made and can make an impact this way also. Recognizing that the Christ is alive in me (one who longs to know Him more deeply) and being with another (who also longs to know God more deeply) is the route. This is the way a legacy is left behind: Recognizing hunger.

To the King,
BuddyO

#29

Dear Men,

With our mouths and with our lives, what are we saying to people? Whether teenagers, neighbors, congregations, circles we sit in, or teams we lead… what are we saying?

If this hasn't been a question you have visited (or revisited within the last 12 months), then it's time to put down the handheld device and consider. A friend of mine put it this way last week, "What is the mission?"

To begin, answer this with me: **What is the difference between a disciple and an apostle?** We know there were 12 disciples of Jesus. But how often within the four Gospels were they called **apostles?**

Matthew – once.
Mark – twice.
Luke – five.
John – zero.

Clearly there was an emphasis on being a disciple of Jesus. *A disciple is an apprentice, one who studies the movements, methods and message <u>of the life</u> of his master.*

I once thought about working on a lathe a few years ago, so I visited a woodworker in Cosby, Tennessee. He had been appointed by the National Park Service to make 75 replica rocking chairs for the 75th anniversary of the Great Smoky Mountains National Park. The learning curve could be quicker, I thought, if I went straight to the best. So, I arrived unexpected, knocked on the door of his shop and was warmly greeted. Before long I had a sharp-ass gouge in my hand and was "turning" a rolling pin out of a crude piece of wood.

That was the last I saw of the craftsman. I realized that I didn't have the deep desire it took to learn the movements, methods and message of the life of this man. Countless hours it would've taken... being his disciple.

An apostle is one who opens his own business... one who has a designated goal, target, hope or mission.

Word spread of the resurrected Savior because Jesus sent His eleven apprentices/disciples (now apostles) to make even more disciples. The mission of the apostles was clear. And we are witnesses to that mission.

But notice that He did not send eleven podcasts or eleven bibles. He sent eleven people. He sent eleven lives with eleven mouths. And He did not (at least in the Great Commission of Matthew 28) send them to a specific location. Instead, I imagine these eleven guys (after Jesus went to heaven) sitting at a picnic table, hashing out what this looked like for each of them.

And by the way, the hashing is part of the going.
(I think this is the best sentence I have written so far)
The hashing is part of the going.
And so is waiting.
Both are part and parcel to being an apostle.

The word "mission" has become overly used and is has grown stale. It has become task-oriented and talent-driven instead of relationally-centered. It is used more as a defining of who I am instead of a result of Who I know. There is a reason we must first be (and then continually be) a disciple. Apostleship latches on.

So, let me end by rephrasing:
What is your relational mission?

For some of us, this question is halting. For some, it is clear. If you'd like to hash, just write back or call. I'm on the other end waiting.

To the King,
BuddyO

#30

Dear Men,

We have not arrived yet. And we will not until heaven comes to earth.
And since we haven't arrived, we cannot (until then) use a past-tense language such as:

- I have learned...
- I understand now that...
- I see the truth in...
- I get it.

But we CAN live in the "ing".

- I am learning.
- I am understanding.
- I am seeing.
- I am beginning to get it.

With that in mind, I'd like to offer a few "Increas<u>ingly</u>" questions that I have been ponder<u>ing</u>.

When you are having coffee with an adult, are you increasingly aware that, not only are you bringing the presence of Christ to him, but he is bringing the presence of Christ to you?

Do you find yourself increasingly having a vision for others? Not just "I wish he would grow up!", but a picture of what he might look like as he steps into being alive to Christ.

Are you increasingly going to bed tired from the energy released from you as you truly connect with God through prayer and with others in relating? Or is this tiredness from semi-relating... a sort of way of using others to advance something you are in charge of?

Are you increasingly drawn (even if it's painful) to the rebels in your life... those who don't see things the way you do or pull against the wonderful momentum you are trying to gain?

Even when clarity is a far-off dream, do you find yourself increasingly leaning (not fully leaning, because we can't yet, remember?) toward a release into God's desire?

Is there an increasing sadness that you've gone another day without your soul being still with God for a period of time... you know, your SOUL sitting still, even though you may have had an obligatory prayer time or scripture reading?

Is there an increasing joy in realizing that others have no need to follow you... that their full need has been met in the only Gospel and that it is your privilege to show up in their beautifully terrible lives without any other agenda than love?

As you get in greater touch with your aging, do you increasingly hear the words, "it's not about me"?

Not yet completely,
but I am living in the ING with you,,

To the King,
BuddyO

#31

Dear Men,

Well, here it is...
The ten percent of our year wrapped into what we call Thanksgiving, Christmas and New Year's. It's an annual event where everything relational gets tossed into the air and we watch to see where and how it lands.

Traditions, past hurts, pushing-through-it, hope, disappointment, memories, avoidance, spousal arguments, crowded schedule, withdrawal, financial adjustments, nostalgia, modified diets, what might have been, what could be, what didn't happen, open arms, closed minds, unspoken sentiments, holes that can't be filled, dreams of new ways of relating, failure, predictable patterns AND we put a tree in the house!

Ninety percent of my year is slow enough (not slow, just slower) to see the iceberg tip of my self-obsession when it comes to connecting. Throughout the year I discover how cold I can be and begin to establish new ways of being present to those I love and new ways of moving toward those I don't. With fresh footing I feel as though a small bit of maturity might be coming my way.

Then, somewhere in late-November, the iceberg quakes and I am rolled into the sea. This season is a terrible and wonderful exercise for those of us who long to be like Jesus.

My **word** for this 10% just hit me.
One word to consider for this season of possibility.
It is a word absent from my everyday vernacular but is recognized as a part of this time of year.

Swaddled.

Relationally, this is NOT the time of year when I feel swaddled, wrapped, encased, cared for, protected, incubated, warmed and nurtured. Instead I feel exposed, foolish, inept, frustrated, weak, short-sited, disjointed and impotent.

Yet, my feelings are not my reality.
In the midst of this crazy time and my yet-to-be-unearthed selfishness I am still swaddled.
I am in Christ.

May this time of year bring you much discovery and joy because of it.

To the King,
BuddyO

#32

Dear Men,

Each of us just had an annual experience called Thanksgiving that was unique to us alone. The people with whom I sat at the table, talked on the phone, longed for, wrote notes to or simply thought about… are mine. Or better said, they are given to me by God.

Each God-made human and every relationship has been placed before me by God. Unless God (for His cosmic reasons) pulls His hands back as He did with Job, allowing Satan to bring these relationships to me, then it is God alone who DEEDS these people to me.

While it is <u>love</u> that chiefly characterizes the person of God, it is <u>hope</u> that characterizes His actions toward/with/for me. And it is in this very hope that I be like His Son in every way that He awards me one another… which includes you.

Take a minute to jot down the names of those that seem to be more of a pain than a gift.
As we move deeper into the ten percent time of year, consider them deeded to you.

To the King,
BuddyO

#33

Dear Men,

For most of my days I have kept a running list in my head. It's a list of things that drive the way I interact and connect with others. And most of these ways are, of course, self-protective.

At the top of that list (not like head-of-the-class, more like I-operate-out-of-this-one-the-most) is this: I don't want to appear dumb.

It takes many forms...
- Kathie offers to help me do a simple task around the house, and I react like I am being treated like a child.
- I sit in a circle of intelligent men, and I find myself crafting what I might say next.
- Conversation with friends turns toward the job security of a local football coach and I weigh in with an ever so insightful reflection.
- A friend casually wonders how I have been spending my time, and I respond with a justification of my "packed" schedule.

I doubt this list will ever shrink or disappear.
I doubt God will use my life while these self-centered relational ways remain within me.
I doubt He will ever save me from the fear of being threatened. After living this way for this long, I often doubt that He even notices.

I receive a little comfort in this Season with two hidden words in the last chapter of Matthew. Jesus told His remaining eleven disciples to go to a mountain in Galilee where He would meet them in resurrected body. They do. Then, just before Jesus gave these specific men the charge to take the Greatest News of all time to the world (The Great Commission)... Matthew writes these simple words:

"When they saw Him, they worshipped Him; but some doubted."

Sandwiched between seeing their risen-from-the-dead Friend and Savior and words-of-vision-for-their-future are these two words... worship & doubt.

While I live a life of doubt with my questions and skepticism, confusion and fears, may I know (may you know) how to worship on Monday through Saturday... with our lives!

To the King,
BuddyO

#34

Dear Men,

There is a First Rule by Anne Lamott when it comes to the discipline of writing.

Butt in Chair.

So, this morning, after prayers and scripture meditation, I write without a dominatingly-profound-thought or moment-of-encounter poised on the tips of my fingers. I sit here pecking away at the keyboard, almost waiting for something to arise within me to say to you that would matter.

Without apologizing, I say: I like mattering. There is a potency rooted deeply in me to make a difference, to move into another, to sprinkle some protein into your soul. Was Adam not crafted this way? Wasn't Paul one bodacious man set on relational-mission to so many people in so many towns? And me?

Within each man is planted this characteristic of God – to have significance in another's life. Meanwhile mattering can be the greatest of all temptations for us! When on Young Life staff several years ago, I remember the urge to be thrilling EVERY DAY. I would not have identified it as "thrilling" back then, but I remember having SUCH a desire to be SO impactful that I proceeded to act more than live.

There lies a great tension between living the life I've been given and fake-it-till-you-make-it, a popular encouragement for this day and time. One is difficult and the other is a lie. One requires a trust that I have never known, one leaves it up to me. One is Godly-relating and the other is not.

Acting tempts me to perform, analyze, measure, produce, balance and scrutinize.

Making an impact for Christ as a unique man creates opportunities for God to have His way in both my life and the life of another... mattering.

May the power of the risen Savior help us.
And as the prayer of old says:
Lord, have mercy, Christ have mercy... as we live in this tension.

To the King,
BuddyO

#35

Dear Men,

How does this happen?

Yesterday, I was a college flunky trying to stay in school and get a degree for I-don't-know-why. And now I sit here late at night in bed while three kids, two daughters-in-law, and three grandkids are under roof along with my wife of 35 years soundly asleep beside me. And it's two nights before Christmas. Yes, the stockings are hung by the chimney with care and nostalgia tries to dominate these last few days... but I can't seem to focus.

What rules me at this time is: How did this happen so fast?

In this moment the impact of flying-time is not simply one of fear. It's more like I am tasting the blurring together of eternal time. Last Christmas happened just a month ago, right? It can't be over 12 years now that Lee Scruggs died, can it?

Even if only briefly, the revisiting of Holy-days helps me slow down to consider this: Time will eventually stop. And I will live in pureness with those whom God has given me today. **Fast** will not be in my vocabulary. Nor will **change**. More importantly, **strife** will be unheard of.

Is there a possibility that relational **strife** and all its' cousins (anger, resentment, hurt feelings, memories of neglect, superiority, etc.) could move toward the exit door while I am still here? Could my love really increase and my anger dissipate? Am I able to cease living from season to season in hope that I might actually stop hiding in the bathroom while waiting on the obligatory family gathering to end so I can, damn it, have my space back?

Last week I had a conversation with my mom... one that I thought would never happen. It was born of a foolishness that created yet another opportunity. But this time I didn't hide, shrink back or body slam her. Instead, with a secure vision for who she and I could be together, I went to an unvisited place with her. Things certainly could've gone south, but there were clear signs pointing true north.

Increasingly, I believe it is happening. While there is no arrival until time stops in that last season called eternity, there IS a blurring together of this quick life and tomorrow's forever. Just the act of me writing this letter to you is a part of this strife ending blur. He has given you to me and me to you. He has given us specific people called Family. And He has charged us with living in hope. And living in love.

May you know His peace on this Christmas Eve day,

To the King,
BuddyO

#36

Dear Men,

I attended another funeral yesterday. The beloved mother/granny of a large family passed over the Christmas season, leaving a big hole for each family member. At the receiving-of-friends there was an expected atmosphere… grief mixed with loss mixed with reunion mixed with a mild disorientation.

I watched several of my friends (members of the family) kindly welcome and greet each of us. With grace they allowed us to say the silly things we say: She was a good one. If I can do anything, just let me know. She is having a better Christmas than we are.

While unthoughtful comments are ill-advised, somehow the accumulation of them brings some comfort. Usually there are enough simple "I am so sorry" statements to wash away all the others. But more importantly, the friends that speak these things <u>belong</u> to those in deep grief.

At a Young Life training workshop in college a speaker said something that would forever shape me. "There are two kinds of people that live in this world" she said. "One who walks into the room and says, 'Here I am!' The other kind of person walks into the room and says, 'There you are!'" During that message almost 40 years ago I began to realize that, while I acted more like that first person, my heart was much more inclined to be a *"There you are!"* person.

But for the first time I am allowing myself to see that there are more than two kinds of people. There are those in the room that have been inflicted. There are those who feel separated from me. There are those who are confused, maturing, can't-stop-eating, contented, hiding, over-it, deflecting, warm, cold, in-a-hole, prayerful, resigned and so on.

And I am beginning to see that there is a third person who walks in the room to say,
Here we are.

This third person is inclusive of all pain and grief, of sinners and sinned-against. While in a conversation with a friend over coffee they include the other while not excluding themselves. All things are allowed even though all things are not understood. But the distinct difference in a **Here we are** person is this: they know that the "we" includes the unpredictable but dependable Spirit of God.

This is who I deeply want to be. One who is not always (can I say this?) about the other, but one who has the Christ and belongs in relationship with another. One who is not there to help, but who is present to the One who lives in each person in the room… including self. I want to recognize the often-times-disruptive and always-loving Spirit of the living and active God.

May we go today not primarily being about the other but about the One.

To the King,
BuddyO

#37

Dear Men,

I have a default setting that I too often and too easily yield to. I like to explain things... especially when it comes to the way I (or others) relate. This is not a bad thing, until it replaces the better thing, which happens a lot.

Earlier this morning I wrote a completely different #37. Rarely do I read it to another before sending it to you, but for some reason I did. After hearing it my friend didn't respond directly about what I wrote. Instead, he spoke about what awoke within him as he listened. While he was speaking to me I became aware that my email was more about explaining why we relate – More of a diagram than an invitation to something deeper.

Again, not a bad thing. Friends and therapists often explain people dynamics and help us understand relational stuff that goos on underneath our surface. I have many friends who are professionals in the counseling world... sharp, prayerful and insightful folks who long for others to walk in the grace of God that is already given. *Please God, may we all be attentive to the personal ways in which we connect with one another!*

But there is a better thing. And my friend spoke of this *better thing* this morning. He did not feel (or yield to) the common pull to agree or disagree with my "explanations". Instead he spoke of a very alive **HOPE** stirring in him.

Not only was this better hope a growing and active energy within him, it also opened up a place in the conversation that allowed me to be with him. Nothing to debate or determine. No principle to get in step with. No trying to explain "what went wrong". Just a friendship that offered a "what might be".

Oh, that my default toward hope was more ingrained within me. But wait, it is!

The Amish calls our God – The Great Within.
And that is where our hope is anchored. Anchored in a Person living in me and you. One called The Holy Spirit.

Well, there I go explaining again. Not a bad thing. But I am hungry for more than understanding... I'm longing for the Person. And I want to increasingly put my hope in Him. That's the better Hope.

To the King,
BuddyO

#38

Dear Men,

You can ask Kathie, "What is Buddy's favorite thing?" and I bet she'll nail it every time. I can hear her now...

He loves for someone to make him a sandwich.

There is, of course, more underneath that statement. If you make me a sandwich, you stop and wonder... what would he like? Should I make ham or turkey? Does he like yellow mustard or stone-ground? Bread... Kaiser, wheat, sourdough?

In other words, you think about me.
And I love that. It's my favorite thing... to be thought about.

Well, last week a good friend made me a sandwich by sending a podcast. Here is how the sandwich was constructed.

My friend, Jim Branch, sent me a link to an interview of
Eugene Peterson who spoke of being influenced by
Karl Barth who halted me with statement on
Prayer.

Peterson says, "If we pray without listening, we pray out of context. The listening business is the part of prayer that gets most neglected. One of the best teachers for me in this has been Karl Barth... and he was just adamant about – when you pray, you don't ask God for things. You pray to listen. And then, when you've listened, you can hear God speak and take you into paths you never thought about."

I paused the podcast and thought – why does this taste so good? Listening as prayer is not a foreign thought, but this is sticking to my ribs! As I digested this paragraph a bit more it occurred to me that, in regards to prayer, the pressure is off! No pressure to come up with:

What does God want me to say?
How does He want me to say it?
Have I included enough praise and gratitude in my prayers?
Are my good thoughts about someone the same as praying for them?
How much selfishness is laced in my prayers?
Are my prayers ignored completely, partially or none at all?
Could my prayers be heard more if I use an aid like the Book of Common Prayer?
Is my discouragement linked to my lack of said-prayers?
How and where do I begin?

"The listening business is the part of prayer that gets most neglected." And Peterson goes on to say, "God speaks to us… our answers are our prayers."

Much for me to chew on.

But maybe my favorite thing is actually this… to make a sandwich for another.
The link is OnBeing.org

Thanks Jim.

To the King,
BuddyO

#39

Dear Men,

On a scale of 1-10 regarding OCD, I am about an eight. I love how the great American poet, Billy Collins, puts it in the opening verses of *The Straightener*.

Even as a boy I was a straightener.
On a long table near my window
I kept a lantern, a spyglass, and my tomahawk.

Never tomahawk, lantern and spyglass.
Always lantern spyglass, tomahawk.

You could never tell when you would need them,
but that was the order that you would need them in.

I'm the same with numbers. At times I can remember birthdays and phone numbers better than someone's name. All this is to say: This #39 must be written about my Dad who died at the same age.

I was ten years old and just started the sixth grade. A few days before he died from cancer, I remember crying in the bathroom at Chilhowee Elementary school. I was taking a leak in one of those tall urinals that went all the way to the floor. Normally I would make designs, but this time I just stood and wept openly. Behind me there was, of course, a fair dose of bullying. (In hindsight I should've swung around and pissed all over them.) But that day my tears seemed to cool their jets enough, because in retaliation I said, *You'd cry too if your Dad was dying!*

Although he holstered a mean belt and a fiery temper, I somehow remember him well. Maybe because we didn't go through my puberty together or never got to the point of wondering if I would join the family construction business. And I never wrecked his Oldsmobile. Which leads me to what I miss:

We never collided.

When my boys were younger we would wrestle on the rug. I knew then and know now that it was just an excuse to hug. But as they aged into acne and whiskers, I still loved it. There still remained this need to "collide" with them, if for no other reason than to just hold each other.

Yep, most collisions are ugly. But necessary. While we discover what ticks us off, we also unearth coping mechanisms, avoidance techniques and default settings. By colliding, we find out a lot about ourselves.

But more than anything else, the sheer lack of growing up without a dad opened my eyes wide to the desire for one. For we were made to be loved. But more so, as I like to remind us, we were made <u>to love</u>. We were made to look beyond what we didn't get, what can't have, what our deficiencies are... and love instead. We were not made to talk about love (or the lack of it), we were made to consider the driver to our left and the woman that shares our bed. We were not created to keep score or count calories, speak truth or regurgitate scripture, be seen or have community. We were made to actively, thoughtfully, covertly, happily, carefully, increasingly see another and love them.

And we were made to listen to our Father and hear Him say, *I'm not going anywhere with my love. Here I will stay. You were made for this and nothing more. Now go as I have.*

To the King,
BuddyO

#40

Dear Men,

As we seek to live a life of following Jesus, there are many words/ideas repeated. Many of these words are spoken to us and some are even uttered by us. Meaningful words such as hope, prayer, sympathy, love, neighbor, vision, etc. But there is one word that gets lost in the shuffle because it seems to require an extra amount of ummph that is difficult to find. The word is:

Review

Here I am talking about the ancient practice of surveying my interior and exterior world of the relational sin that so easily bogs me down. I know I got it, I know I need to confess it, and I know that all this precludes repentance… but, for me, it does not happen simply.

Apart from a dogged discipline, it seems hard to imagine that a review of my life will actually take place with great regularity. Inspection and analysis of my motivations (especially at the end of my day) seems both exhausting and derailing. And with the certainty of its necessity and the sure pardon of sin, I still can't seem to muster the…is it energy?... to look in the mirror.

I have been away with five peers for the last thirty hours. It's an annual event that I, to be frank, drag my feet into as the January retreat approaches. Each person is given one hour to update, process, vomit, expose, dream… in other words, **review** their own life in front of the others.

What did I discover more about Buddy from this simple overnight?

- While he is slow to move from the place he has been given, he gets caught up in his own little cares in his own little world.
- He thinks a lot about aging.

- Jesus can be a means to him instead of just allowing Jesus to be Jesus.
- In his listening, **solving** is still difficult to avoid.
- The dragging of his feet exposes his reluctance to reveal some deeper hopes he carries.
- Speaking of hope, he hopes more than he knows.
- He still likes to laugh.
- He likes a good meal.
- And loving is his greatest desire.

Needed **review** came more readily when I showed up looking for Jesus in another. And the energy it took barely registered on the meter.

May I suggest a short task?

- Do this: Pick up the phone or write a letter to a friend (or two).
- Say this: "I need to hear some things. (And so do you). Could we have coffee every week for about thirty years?"
- Remember this: You will be disappointed.

If you already do this with a few guys, here is your next assignment:

- Do this: Show up on time at your next coffee.
- Say this: "I need to live with less crap in my inner world. (And so do you). At the risk of being too navel-gazing, would you listen more intently to me and ask the same of me in return?"
- Remember this: You will be disappointed.

But do it anyway.
Thirty hours, thirty days or thirty years will prove one thing... Jesus comes to us upon invitation.

To the King,
BuddyO

#41

Dear Men,

This short letter is meant to invite you more deeply into the geography of tension.

I had another enjoyable conversation with a friend not long ago and The Wizard of Oz came up. You know, that extraordinary and scary television tale of our youth. I remember running to my bedroom as a kid when the witch showed up on the roof to hurl fireballs at the Tin Man.

At the end of the movie when Dorothy woke up from a bump on the head, she kept pleading with Auntie Em that she didn't have a nightmare. "It wasn't a dream. It was a place... a real, truly live place. I remember that some of it wasn't very nice. But most of it was beautiful!"

Men, we are not from this planet. Many of us are spending way too much time thinking about the direction our country is headed and worried about the waves of discontent in America. We lay blame, draw lines in the sand, stand up in solidarity for our rights and fret ourselves into a nightmare. There are a lot of not very nice things going on. Many of them called injustice.

But we have forgotten that we are not from here. Here on earth we cannot find what we are looking for... no more than the Scarecrow can gain knowledge by obtaining a rolled up piece of paper.

This planet offers nothing but the following promises ala Frank Baum:
- Today you and I live in a real, truly live place.
- Frightening things happen all around us.
- Most of it is beautiful!
- Especially those characters that show up in your life.
- It is not our home. He is.

Jesus says many of the same things, but adds:

- When all these beautiful characters I have given you (your co-worker, wife, neighbor-you-have-not-yet-met, grocery lady, father-in-law, postman, children, butcher, baker and candlestick maker) see THAT YOU LOVE like I love you, then they will all know that you belong to Me. They won't see that until you love them.
- I live in you also… giving you no more and no less than just what you need to love ALL these beauties I have given you.
- Meanwhile you live in the geography of tension between this place that I have put you and your true home. And someday I will come to you and you will make your home with Me, your true home and you will say as Dorothy said:

We're home!
And this is my room.
And you're all here.
And I'm not going to leave here ever, ever again because I love you all.

Here's to courage, heart and knowledge of the person of Jesus!

To the King,
BuddyO

#42

Dear Men,

Eugene Peterson's life has shaped me more than any author. But even after reading <u>several</u> of his books I find myself profoundly impacted by a little podcast with him (see #38).

Peterson memorizes poems. Yep, you heard me correctly... this octogenarian spends his declining brain cells and swiftly-moving-calendar taking the words of poets and locking them in his mind. And he encourages us to practice this also. Why? Why would I spend the incredible amount of time it takes to do memory-roll with a single and proper sequence of words until they are branded into my psyche? And is there something weighty that poets are saying that the scriptures do not?

No. It is not about the words. Peterson says, "Find a few artists and study their language." It is not simply about what they are saying or even how they say it. It is about knowing the artist.

Since I am married to an artist I could show you ten ways Kathie holds her brush. I could show you ten ways she pulls or pushes that brush with ten different pressures. Add to that the way she mixes a myriad of colors on the palette or sees lavender in the February treetops, dappled light on a distant forest floor or the bouncing blue of the sky reflecting from a cow's back.

I began this paragraph improperly with "Since I am married to an artist". Participating in a wedding ceremony or sleeping in the same bed with an artist does not help me to know her. Looking at her paintings, as wonderful as they are, do not help me know her very well either. But, somehow, studying her ways of seeing a hillside or dancing on the canvas with a brush allows me entrance into her.

Many artists say they are trying to tell a story when they paint. Well, the story they are trying to communicate is not within the canvas as much as it is in the hand... they are telling THEIR story.

This is a game changer. Studying the language of poets (Lucy Shaw, King David or Billy Collins), artists (Kathie Odom, Mark Boedges or Joaquin Sorrola) or musicians (Jackson Browne, Bill MIze or Bono) helps me see and be with others. It's not about what they are saying, painting or singing. It's about them.

That person across the table from you... you know the one. They do not need fixing or correction. They are speaking, sitting and sipping coffee in ways that point to their journey. Study them, not in an intellectual way but in a soulful way, for they are a redeemed soul.

May my game change, Lord? May I know you by studying Your language? Seeing You which includes Your words. May I know Your ways not to simply imitate them, but to know You, the only true God and Jesus Christ whom You have sent.

To the King,
BuddyO

#43

Dear Men,

Yesterday I wore a red cap and a Cardinal's T-shirt as Dad watched from the concrete bleachers. My first base hit.
Yesterday I avoided David Higdon but it didn't work. My first fist-fight.
Yesterday I misspelled a-x-l-e. My first spelling bee.
Yesterday I saw Hawaii on the big screen. My first movie.
Yesterday I sat motionless as Mom spoke the impossible words to me. My first funeral.
Yesterday I raced home to watch Gilligan. My first friend.
Last Monday I was late to Boy Scouts. My first family.

Yesterday I had a bedtime, a train set and a secret hiding place. Red Skelton was king.

Then came cutting class, pitching pennies, wet dreams and cigarettes.
Zero Bars.
Summer pool.
Chigger bites.
Slate Rock Hill.
Banjo lessons.
Schwinn Bikes.
First paycheck, first dance, first kiss, first wreck.
All that happened Yesterday.

I met before the student disciplinary board, directed traffic on Cumberland, learned a G chord, saw Eric Clapton and Muddy Waters up close for eight bucks, met the girl, leapt the Andy Holt steps two-at-a-time on the way to heaven, discovered belly-laughs and teenagers and faith.

It's easy to remember because it
Was all Yesterday.

Somewhere in there I was embraced by a people, held to account by a man, received a new name from a woman, and was given a lot of responsibility.

Somewhere in there I was late, showed up early, disappointed others, surprised a few, became the fool, drank the Kool-aid, crossed the line and walked a dog.

Yesterday someone counted on me.
Yesterday someone looked for me.
Yesterday my fourth grandchild was born.

Wendell Berry writes...

> The young man leaps, and lands
> On an old man's legs.

Keep jumping fellas.

To the King,
BuddyO

#44

Dear Men,

Because I was made to love God and others, I write.

It is my way of working love out. It is my way of sorting through all the million words and thoughts that come to me throughout each given day. It is my way of ciphering my existence. In writing I filter conversations and books, questions and quotes, intentions and failures, temptations and memories... all for the sole purpose of learning to love, learning to be me.

Loving is my greatest desire. Yours too, whether you know it or not. And, quite often as I write, I end up asking –since loving is my greatest desire, **how can I love better?**

As much as I ask this, I continue to return to only one door with one key. The door to loving won't budge and neither will I in my loving... without the key. Loving greatly is not as simplistic as putting your hand on the doorknob and turning it... it's not just choosing to be nice in the presence of un-nice-ness. It is not A + B = C.

First the key to this five-word question, **how can I love better?** The key is this: There is no I in the question. The door to loving God and others is un-openable without a deeply growing and embedded knowledge of this... there is no longer an I in – **how can I love better?** There is now for those who are in Christ Jesus only a We.

He and I sit together in my kitchen right now with fingers on the computer. We (mostly unaware to me) are sifting, sorting and ciphering out our existence together. Not only am I not-alone (left as an orphan, Jesus said) but He and I are one! I will never be an I. Never. All that is asked of me is asked of we. All courage needed, insight desired, steadiness hoped for and gumption required to love another is found in the we.

This key is so beautiful and extraordinary that I might be tempted to simply spend my life turning the key back and forth, back and forth. Monks commit their remaining days to this sort of back and forth awe and contemplation... that God in Christ has taken up residence within sinners. But now I (we) am able to push against the door.

If the key is **there is no I,** then what is the door to **how can I love better?**
Answer: Reviewing how I relate.
This is why I write these letters. I am working out my love in words and processing truckloads of stimuli by asking **how am I relating?**

To God, Kathie, Kenny across the street, the associate pastor, the tattooed Starbucks teenager, my mom, her brother, my barber, peers who act juvenile, kids living next door, mechanics that charge too much, encroaching in-laws, mentors, panhandlers, children, big dude in small Delta seat across the aisle from me, woman-I-called-for-insurance-help-but-instead-she-starts-telling-me-how-worried-she-is-for-her-emotionally-challenged-son-in-Kansas-and-that-she-has-an-unscheduled-mamogram-this-afternoon, etc.

The door to loving better is in the question **how am I relating?**
The key to asking this question is **you and I are not orphans**. Not in any stretch of the imagination.

Lord willing, WE will explore more later. And together.

To the King,
BuddyO

#45

Dear Men,

I can't thank you enough for those who reply to one of these letters from time to time. I love the interaction.

It keeps my mind and heart racing alongside each other. You see, my mind tends to run ahead of you with hopes to figure out what you really mean, what's underneath what you are saying, how I may help. But lately, my heart is somehow keeping pace with my mind (barely) enough to remind it to slow down a little bit.

When left to its own devices, the common American mind wants to scrutinize all things personal so it may give resolve to what is at hand (get to the bottom line of the problem). But the truly-Christian mind realizes it does not operate in a vacuum. The mind lives within the soul (which also houses the person's heart, spirit, will, body, etc.) and therefore does not actually have its own devices to rely upon. The mind cannot operate of its own accord... these other influences within the soul cannot be discounted. In other words, the mind and heart were made to keep pace with one another.

Let's look at Randy, a man who loves Jesus. His days are peppered with people and meetings because folks need the One whom he has. Randy deeply desires to spend daily time alone with God for refreshment and prayer which has proved rewarding. He knows that the longings of all creation are only satisfied in a relational God, and realizes that he has been equipped with enough courage to go places where only a few have gone. Randy has tasted the fruit of a long obedience. And he has witnessed his friends wade into their own little worlds with a God-injected trust. His is a life full of quiet miracles and steady people.

But he lives with an intense disquiet-ness. **Scrutiny-of-self** rears its head with regularity. In one ear he hears that self-evaluation is healthy and needed so as to guard the soul from evil ways. So his mind races to the scene to implement an oxymoron – scrutinize his own scrutiny. How am I doing? Am I reviewing my life enough? Am I growing sufficiently to stay in this job? People are counting on me… do they see that I am working hard for both the Lord and them? Are my answers holding up when their faith is weak? Can they see my lingering judgements that I work so hard to hide? Is love winning in me or are these just good habits I've implanted? Am I walking by faith or simply doing really good relational work?

The other ear sings a different tune to the mind, the voice of a godly Jimmy Buffet: **Chill man.** Go be yourself. God's got this. He lives in you and is the Redeemer, so you can't screw this up as much as you think. Be real and let others identify with your pain like David did in the Psalms. Wake up tomorrow like you went to bed… forgiven.

Randy is thinking – What ear should I listen to? And the common answer (because he has a full life that needs attention) is compartmentalization… the result of a mind being left to its own devices (again, as if it has its own devices). But compartmentalization keeps the soul from engaging because the busy mind has opted instead for some peace. But Randy knows that is only temporary. He knows there will come a day when tragedy shatters all his orderly compartments.

So, when I am met with this intense disquiet-ness within myself to **figure life out**, how do I engage my whole self, my soul? When I read something convicting or taste a moment of beauty… how do I open my entire self to God without wanting to sell it, teach it or freeze it for later?

The Season of Lent approaches in a couple days. Ash Wednesday becomes a common starting block for many people to open their souls up to God. May I suggest something? Spend 40 days (not Sundays) trying a new practice:

Until Easter Sunday construct a small daily habit around **Confession**.

Come up with some way of living more regularly with the act of confessing what you know, what you don't know and what you don't want to know.

I remember committing ten minutes a day in silent confession for Lent one year. It was a struggle to take 600 seconds per day to think on and admit how I lived for myself. Then it hit me that I needed to confess that I don't even SEE how I lived so much for me. It was then that the floodgates seemed to open.

How may we consider confession, Oh Lord, to be a help to us to know You?

To the King,
BuddyO

#46

Dear Men,

I ended last week's letter with an invitation to consider **Confession**... specifically to construct a small daily habit during the Lenten season around it.

I admit that I am actually **considering** it more than practicing it. There have been a few moments when I reviewed the day or the encounter with another person and asked myself (in so many words or thoughts), "how did I do?". In doing so I have picked through the small haystacks within myself and have, no doubt, discovered selfish ways worthy of contrite admission to God.

But as I **consider confession** (vs. practice it) something like the following arise within me:

At this age, my body hurts so much.
I wonder how long I will live.
What will be the cause of my death?
Anyone under the age of 50 dismisses most of what there is about aging.
Everyone over fifty smells what I'm stepping in.
How will I leave Kathie financially and emotionally when I die? (or me, if she dies first?)
It will feel like 2000 pounds of brick on my chest when she passes.
Will I work hard to be a strong model for friends after she is gone, or just come what may?
Will I speak at her funeral?
Time flies.
While it helps me sleep more soundly, I have moments where I drink a little too much wine.
Or am I just longing to relax my body from the accumulation of relationships that take a toll?
I wish I hadn't written that.
Well, there's the backspace key, pal.
It will make me look brave and humble to leave it.

Ponder something else.
My life is full of so much beauty and I want for no more.
So why do I reside in the ache of life so much? And the life that is yet to come before I die?
Ah, to have half the wisdom Kathie has... and that is no hyperbole.
Wisdom to shut up. To see.
To offer space that emits from an open heart instead of an open calendar.
To drink more good fruit than fermented.
To drink the fermented with an anticipated enjoyment.
To allow questions to settle within me.
To acknowledge the miracle it is that she has potency.
To rightly credit a life of being carried vs. making bright decisions.

This is just a tiny, tiny amount of what it has meant to **consider** confession this week.
To the King,
BuddyO

#47

Dear Men,

I wrote in #44:
"There is no longer an I in – **how can I love better?** There is now for those who are in Christ Jesus only a We." This, my friends, is being/thinking/living a Trinitarian theology.

My wager is that every single one of us, if asked, would say that we have a Trinitarian theology. Each of us have a *reasoning* of God that is not only shaped by a Three-in-One Deity but is also personal. We believe that God the Father is one with Jesus the Son is one with the indwelling Holy Spirit. We believe that the Son came from the Father to show us what He is like and to return to the Father but not leave us alone… He set up a new home for Himself within us. Yes, this is a Trinitarian Theology.

But does it make a difference?

Seeing this question – *But does it make a difference?* – as one to answer, will lead us back to the dangerous Scrutiny-of-self question of performance – *How am I doing?*

But seeing this question – *But does it make a difference?* – as one to swim in, will lead us in grace to wonder about the ways our Trinitarian God (notice, I didn't just say *God*) impacts my interior world which leads to impacting other's interior worlds.

Answering vs. Swimming.
Hmmm.

All of you know me to some degree. If you know me very well, you know that my background is not impressive regarding the study or reasoning on the study of anything. Yet, when it comes to swimming I have a yellow ribbon.

There were three eight-year-olds taking swim lessons at the downtown YMCA in 1965. After one week we had a contest to see who could hold their breath the longest and float "like a jellyfish". Second place for me. Yellow ribbon. Proof that I can swim.

Dear Men, it is not possible to understand the entirety of our Trinitarian God any more than it is to drink the ocean. But we CAN swim in it!

Wondering if a Trinitarian Theology makes a difference vs. grading my progress on how well I am keeping a Trinitarian Theology will help each of us live in the love of God instead of getting-ahead-of or on-top-of the love of God.

A good friend wrote this to me:

'How can I love better?' makes me feel like I need to do more… do better at something… earn it. Even though it's about people, it feels task-oriented. *'How am I relating?'* feels people-oriented.

When we find ourselves keeping a personal scorecard less and less, we will find that we are living a Trinitarian Theology by the way in which we relate with others.

THAT is freedom.
THAT is living in grace.
THAT is a Trinitarian Theology.
And THAT makes a difference.

To the King,
BuddyO

#48

Dear Men,

This morning I read that Nathaniel Hawthorne published the first great American novel on this day in 1850. In reading the excerpt below I thought about how I often move about in life. Read this paragraph and I'll reflect afterwards.

*Hawthorne thought **The Scarlett Letter** was too bleak to be published by itself, and he planned to include it in a collection with a few other short stories. His publisher thought it was good enough to stand alone, but Hawthorne still had doubts about it. He wrote: "Is it safe, then, to stake the fate of the entire book entirely on this one chance? A hunter loads his gun with a bullet and several buck-shot. ... It was my purpose to conjoin the one long story with half a dozen shorter ones; so that, failing to kill the public outright with my biggest and heaviest lump of lead, I might have other chances with the smaller bits."*

It occurs to me that I have rarely staked my life on one sincere bullet of Buddy Odom. Always I have stuffed multiple flavored buckshot down my gun to "preserve" my what? My persona? Some idea of who I want people to think me to be? Some chance to live on if I fail? An opportunity to at least stay in the game if I don't win or draw first blood?

Therefore, I have had (at least in my mind and sometimes in actuality) great success at staying ambiguous and distant, controlling collateral damage, avoiding the possibility of relational bankruptcy with another, standing on the sideline, appearing wise and recruiting lots of people to one day attend my funeral.

But in doing so I have failed to give my truest self, my possibly-most-loving-self to others.

No Nathaniel, it <u>IS NOT</u> safe to stake the fate of Buddy Odom on one bullet.

But it's all I really have... this one single shot called me.

... with our Triune God living within. How can I miss?

You might be interested in joining me with this prayer...
My Lord, May I no longer seek to first relationally hedge my bets or soften the blow.
May I live more deeply from my soul instead of only my mind.
May I not play out scenarios in my head in advance of connecting with others which often results in NOT connecting with others.
May I more easily and quickly give whatever one shot of my truest (Christ-est) self that is loaded in the barrel.
And wrap it in love, my Lord, allowing it to be our best shot together. Amen.

To the King,
BuddyO

#49

Dear Men,

There seem to be three different categories of people in my life... those I choose to be around, those I would never choose to be around and those I choose to not be around. I'd like to explore the group that I overlook the most... *those I would never choose to be around.*

It's not because I don't like them (that's the third group). These folks fall into the middle group because they are the most invisible to me. Acquaintances, co-workers, grocery check-out ladies, friends-of-friends, family-of-friends, clients, members of other circles, people unlike me, etc. Again, it's NOT that I don't like them, it's just that I never make the choice to be around them.

Logically, we have a finite amount of capacity, right? We can't care deeply when we are relationally a mile wide and an inch deep. But how do I end up relating with these people whom God has brought into my path?

To keep myself from just hustling through the day, my most common style of relating is to implement well-thought-out strategies to keep these folks from becoming invisible... looking at an employee name badge so I can thank Randy by name when he hands me a mocha, add a touch of get acquainted conversation to a brief encounter, smile and give the hello-nod, bring a little humor to lighten the moment, slow down just enough to "be with" the person in front of me or just be nice today.

ALL of these are very good ways to live. But if the source is purely a strategy, even a thoughtful one like "I don't need to just hustle through my day", then I am not living very open to God. Instead I am living to maintain sanity or carry out a specific mission God has given me (which is different than living with openness to God).

Creating Mission Statements can be dangerous in this way. Developing a game plan can limit our love. Even a strategy to love can be less about keeping these folks from becoming invisible, and more about me managing my own story. How good it would be say thanks to Randy out of an openness that God has given me Randy at this moment!

This may feel like splitting hairs. But review your casual encounters today to see if they are based on management or openness. Slow down enough to review how you look (or don't look) at people, what interior motivations are driving you. If we are attentive today to the ways we relate, we might discover something from God expanding within us... followed by an unplanned smile and hello-nod.

To the King,
BuddyO

#50

Dear Men,

Below is a letter I wrote to a friend after meeting together a couple weeks ago. His name is not Randy. But to all "Randy's" out there, I'm jealous of your name. Thanks for reading.

Dear Randy,
*I left our time somehow **wanting** to feel uneasy because we had spoken so frankly. Very few people talk to me the way you did. Often folks feel the need to be on their game with me, or correction is on the way. Understandable. I can be that way.*

Instead you brought Randy. It felt 90 percent beautiful for you to correct my best writing... diving for the jugular with love in your hand. I thought to myself, who does this? I wanted to feel uneasy, but it didn't last.

I was driving west on I-40 behind an abnormally slow and very used Honda. It was this Slim Shady wannabe flicking his cig ashes out the sunroof. I had our conversation in mind and didn't appreciate his staggering speed that boxed me up against a semi. When I finally freed myself to pass on the right, I glanced over with a well-practiced partial stare. You know, the just-condescending-enough-but-not-condescending-why-are-you-in-my-lane-you-turd-please-and-thank-you look.

He wouldn't look at me. He was in the middle of doing something with a young woman.
I was shocked. And fascinated. But only for a brief moment... they exited onto Papermill Road.

I suddenly felt sick. Sick with my naïveté, sick for her, sick that I wanted to see more. Thoughts of our rich conversation vanished so quickly, Randy. The world jerked my head around, tempting or educating or scolding or enlightening me on what-I-don't-know.

What happened on the interstate lingers in me this morning. Still a little wobbly I walk into the dark kitchen and the memory of our long friendship returns. I am a man living at the top of the food-chain – a rich, white, American male. Apologies, excuses and embarrassments seem in order. But you don't always see me that way. While you know that I love to pass people on the right, you don't hold it against me.

My love to you, BuddyO

Men,
There are people in my life that consider relationships to be the highest order, like the one found in The Trinity. May we be those other-centered friends to one another like Randy is to me.

To the King,
BuddyO

#51

Dear Men,

With great regularity I encounter both men and women who desire deeply to live in Godly community, where the word Family is based on the blood of our Lord. Kathie and I have many friends seeking to fulfill this wonderful desire by living near one another in neighborhoods, caring for one another's kids, going on vacations together, etc.

What are great relationships based on? How do friendships in Christ become a community in Christ? Can you think of a good friend and consider how your friendship came to be?

Maybe you experienced a shared ministry or a brokenness together. Maybe you logged truck-loads of hours together as roommates or college friends. Maybe you bonded over adventure. Time, experiences together, rich conversations and maybe even some hard soul-work formed the foundation that allowed you to be known in ways you'd never before experienced.

And now you, as one who hungers for God, also hunger for more of this sort of living… a life of love with folks in the same stage of life. What a great thing to hope for, pray for and pursue.

Let's take a side-trip at this point. Below are the (partial) lyrics to John Mayer's song, "Love is a Verb". Read them and tell me what seems wrong.

> Love is a verb
> It ain't a thing
> It's not something you own
> It's not something you scream
>
> When you show me love
> I don't need your words
> Yeah love ain't a thing
> Love is a verb

So you gotta show, show, show me
Show, show, show me
Show, show, show me
That love is a verb

Yeah you gotta show, show, show me
Show, show, show me
Show, show, show me
That love is a verb

Do you see the not-so-subtle-yeah-you-gotta-show-me demand in there? When we see and experience a wonderful thing (such as being loved), we can easily begin to require others to keep the good love thing going.

Deeply knowing and loving one another stops being as important as being deeply known and loved.

But, for the Christian there is no one that's <u>gotta</u> show you love.

No friend, no pastor, no spouse, no next-door neighbor, no family member, no mentor, no child. No one. Why? Because someOne already has.

Pray to Hosanna that He would not give you someone to be loved by. Instead, pray to Hosanna that He would give you someone to love.

Oh, wait. He already has….
Your friends, your pastor, your spouse, your next-door neighbor, your Mom, your sister, your mentor, your kids.
Now all you need is courage.
Pray for that.

To the King this happy Easter!
BuddyO

#52

Dear Men,

I thought I'd right you a letter from someone else... just to change things up a bit:

Dear Men,

My name is JT. Buddy is a new friend that I am getting to know and he asked me to write the following letter to you. Says he wants you guys to know me. Not sure why.

I guess it was my parents who first gave me the name Thaddaeus, although I never remember them ever saying my name. My father killed a guy for I-don't-know-why and my mother was then labeled as the wife of a murderer. Guess I just got swept under the rug.

I've never laid eyes on the old man. Growing up with a father in prison made me catch a lot of hell about it from kids in the neighborhood. All the fist fights don't make for a bunch of friendships. I got pretty lonely. Before you knew it I just blended into the background like wallpaper. Sort of invisible. That's where the JT comes from. "Oh, that's Just Thaddaeus."

The last three years have been pretty crazy and confusing. My life took a spin when this guy came to town and, well, how do I say this? He laid His eyes on me. Can't say I ever had anyone actually notice me till then. Not only that. He invited me to be a part of his pack of friends, which were a bunch of misfits in their own right. Loud-mouths, dropouts, some with good jobs, others notsomuch.

As I look back on it now I see that I was (we were) being shown, by the life of this man, that my world ain't just my world. There is something much bigger and includes more people, something more thrilling but real scary. Something even cosmic (I learned that word from Him).

He was an artist. Like with words, I mean. While others quizzed Him on the meaning of a story about a vineyard being rented out to farmers, I closed my eyes and imagined my sweat and muscle-ache. I smelled fresh grapes and the sound of a clacking bucket in my hand as I went to the winepress. It seemed that I was always a part of His story. He never called me JT.

I could talk to you about Him forever because, He seemed strangely lonely. Not like I do with all the pushing back of people and hiding, but more like all of Himself was not quite present. This can't be right because I'd never known someone to laugh so hard who was my kind of lonely. I'd never known someone to be so accepting who was my kind of lonely. I'd never known someone to be so kind-hearted who was my kind of lonely.

And the wildest thing was: He believed in me. ME... an angry hermit of a guy with no future to speak of! He wanted me to be His kind of lonely. A loneliness that was driven by what He called hope. A sadness driven by a kind heart. An inside-out living that was anchored in, what He called, His Father.

I'm gettin' tired just now trying to find words for it all. But it seems like I have to do this. It seems like this whole father-thing has got me Father-searching. And (maybe He knew this about me) – I gotta live my life out loud.

Maybe what happened over these past few days might help me with it all. It's mostly just a big blur. Our group of friends was expanding month by month and then there was an out-of-the-blue raid on us from the damn soldiers and then we were all left without Him and then I heard He was killed and then buried and then, I'm still not sure, but, well... we saw Him.

All I remembered was this. He said, GO.

To me, the one that wants to hide, fight, get revenge, be independent, forget, move on with life, find my own way, ignore others, keep to myself, make decisions alone, blame my father and count on no one else... He says to me GO.

Oh yes, and this too: I WILL BE WITH YOU. Unlike my father, who left with no words or warning, Jesus is still alive in me with this kind-hearted, life-bustin' kind of hope. And I think with a little fire to love others. Like He did with me. With all of us.

You may be real different than me and this letter may show that. But, for some reason, Buddy wanted you to know me. He told me once that we all belong together like God is together Himself. And that we were made to live out loud that way. Unified or Being One, Buddy calls it. Says we have the same Father. While I don't understand, it makes me sort of glad.

Your brother,
Thaddaeus.

#53

Dear Men,

Although I was generally not very good in school, I was great at math, any math. I still love parabola computation, geometry, and figuring out how tall a tree is. I am fascinated with numbers... the home phone number for my high school best friend was 524-1349. There were 17 steps down to my basement at 5512 East Sunset Road.

Because of my junior-level OCD tendencies, I count things. It was more intense several years ago but never debilitating. Kathie knows all this, and last evening I kissed her goodnight with a few words... "Honey, I just realized that we've been married over 13,000 nights".

This came from gratitude. I saw her climb into our king size bed and realized how extraordinary my life is and has been.

You see, yesterday we Sabbathed together. We took time away from busyness... on the scale of 1-10 for productivity, it was about a two. It was a day to guiltlessly subtract all the voices calling us to "make a difference". There was lounging and poached eggs and television and the smell of cut flowers and napping and talking about the rain and a wink and a facetime with the kids.

Yesterday was wonderful, but I confess that I don't honor the fourth commandment as often as my Lord wishes. As He says in Hebrews 4, we are to make every effort to enter that rest made available to us.

We remembered the command to, every seven days, stop creating. Instead we are to re-create. We are to give maintenance to a space (by stopping every seven days) within ourselves that honors quitting. Included in this quitting is rest and remembering. Included in this quitting is, as Eugene Peterson says, playing and praying.

I was greatly impacted by a story from Abraham Heschel years ago. He tells of a rabbi leisurely strolling his property on the Sabbath... taking it real easy and walking with God. He saw a breach in the fence and thought to himself, since it is the Sabbath I will repair that broken fence tomorrow. But then, after realizing how sacred this set-aside-day truly is to God, the rabbi said to himself – since I thought of repairing the fence on the Sabbath, I will NEVER repair it.

How do you rhythmically honor this chosen day? How do you move toward the command to keep these particular 24 hours as holy? To what degree does it register on your importance radar? Does playing and praying feel contradictory to Godly living?

When I kissed Kathie goodnight with the 13,000-night proclomation, both she and I had a moment of wow. A marvel surfaced that may not have if we would've seized the time to pay bills or paint the bedroom on Sunday. I slept with a sense that I might be more ready for next week and the troubles inherent in them.

May my rare obedience provoke both you and I to be more attentive to the breaches in our fences.

To the King,
BuddyO

#54

Dear Men,

I discovered this morning what I thought to be true.

Many mornings I sit at a particular table with a peculiar decaf beverage in a particular Starbucks. Today was no different except a group of six men had taken my space.

At 6:30am in Knoxville, Tennessee you can bet it's a church small group... and it was. Five of the men were in their thirties with probably a tired wife and kids-to-get-ready-for-school at home. Two of the men were completely silent. One was nervously bouncing both legs quietly under the table. And a couple of guys offered a question or opinion every now and again. But the 50+ year old white-headed-clearly-in-charge-facilitator spoke 98% of the words.

I was close enough to glean a few phrases he spoke...

- For welfare, not calamity.
- At what point do we stop pestering God?
- God's overarching desire.
- Piper says...
- Look over the abyss.
- Be more discerning.
- There are a ton of lessons and miraculous stories out there.
- Keller had a great message a couple weeks ago...
- Grace and motivation together.
- Press into your walk with God.
- Work out spiritual warfare a little bit.
- Paralytic on the pallet.
- You need to....

On this unique morning there was a price being paid at home by several because dad had an early meeting – what I consider to be an important meeting. But, instead these men circled up to receive yet another sermon. Clearly I believe an opportunity was missed.

What are we to do in our small groups? How are we to sit with a friend over coffee? When we gather with thirsty believers for an hour, how can we lead one another into being an increasingly God-like man or woman?

Like the 50+ year old white-headed-clearly-in-charge-dude, I have countless thoughts. But my #1 is this: There is a better (much better) definition of **Christian Leadership** than what we see and what we practice.

I was invigorated as the hour at Starbucks progressed because I think the dude basically ran out of breath. Since it was prayer-request time, these guys (including the leg-shaker) took turns opening up… and in many ways began taking the conversation in a beautiful off-track sort of direction. Each guy spoke, each guy wondered with surface questions about deeper hungers, each guy gave it a go. And guess what, the old guy was leaning in. Shoulders dropped. Legs stopped shaking. Chuckles evolved. These redeemed souls were perking into an aliveness.

There are many destructive **Christian Leadership** principles that have found their way into our faith. Sometimes they are blatant like wedding-crashers. But most often they are quiet and subtle like an invisible rust corroding the possibilities of real connection with God and one another.

Think about the dude this week. Think about yourself and the primary relationships in which you are engaged. Reflect on your hopes for leading well and remember some of the lost opportunities. In doing so, may we be surprised by the fact that some of these principles may be right under our noses.

I have one I'll share with you next time, Lord willing,
To the King,
BuddyO

#55

Dear Men,

I've been thinking about the dude from last week's email and, in doing so, continue to run into myself over and over. Oh, the ways in which I have shepherded others poorly in the name of Godly leadership!

I think back to the beginning moments of my new awareness of God's love for me. I came home to the Sunday dinner table after a friend's church retreat in Gatlinburg. I was sixteen years old and had "just met Christ". Sitting there with Mom, older sister and little brother, I decided to tell them about the eternally life-altering event that happened while they slept just 18 hours earlier.

I gave my life to Christ last night.

There. I said it. Or it said itself. Or something just happened that I could not explain. My Mom's response was one short, straight sentence and quite memorable:

Don't over do it.

Wow... what a potentially destructive sort of thing to say to a teenager! But who knows what she was thinking at the time. *Those Presbyterians don't believe what we Methodists do. I lost my husband six years ago and now my son is leaving me. I was just hoping for some quiet before heading back to the grind tomorrow morning.*

While her intentions and love for me were good, her **leadership** was most certainly fear-based.

Last week I wrote: "there are many destructive **Christian Leadership** principles that have found their way into our faith." As I thought about the dude and myself over the past seven days, I have wondered about these subtly corrosive foundational beliefs we have that twist our ways of leading.

The most destructive principle is one that I am potentially guilty of now as I write: Leadership requires a certain level of detachment.

To lead we write, teach, preach, journal, study or sit in circles which requires the use of our minds and other faculties of the soul to help us articulate (either to ourselves or others) what it is that we believe or should believe. In doing so we quite naturally live within a conscious and steady stream of analysis, judgement and assessment. Therefore, it seems that the best way to make advancement on the development of our craft (let's say writing, for example) is to take a birds-eye view that doesn't include the bird.

Write about **we** (as I am doing now) but exclude **me** by explaining the problems of culture, determining the routes of correction and establishing the means of moving forward.

Sounds like the dude. Sounds like me.

Each time I sit at the keyboard I am tempted to write about dilemmas (in this case, leadership) that I have observed around me. Oh so quickly I escape or subtract the realities of my own personal dilemma. Why? Because it feels good.

Through detachment I can look wise, appear to be on my game, lead by example, prove my worth, show my insight, create momentum, back up my point or justify my choices. And when I realize that I have not included myself in the subject at hand, I can craft a humble sentence that recognizes my subtraction while all the while maintaining my reputation.

This is the opposite of the Incarnation.

To the King,
BuddyO

#56

May I begin with a few formal words of apology to the word *Incarnational*... I am very sorry for giving you props only in season. Like the Christmas decorations from the basement, I unpack you with wonder and speak of you with great gesture. Soon, however, you are no longer useful for me and my ways of living. I neatly package you for future conversations and refer to you as one I know, yet my heart is far from you.

Dear Men,
Is this way of living familiar to you? The Incarnation is an anchor to belief in God as Trinity, yet I (we?) have relegated and compartmentalized this tenant of my faith to the Advent season.

The final sentence from last week's letter upended my apple cart. Unaware, I linked the Incarnation to Leadership. My fingers typed, "This is the opposite of the Incarnation" and, frankly, I just sat back and looked at the computer screen and wondered... where did those words come from? For seven days, apples have littered my little world.

The most impactful picture of Incarnational Leadership that I can't shake comes in the person of my own daughter, Katie. Summer of 1997 brought our move to Asheville, NC. I remember greeting Katie at the end of her first day as a third grader, anxious to hear what her new world was like. She replied, "They gave me Amber".

Completely blind was this fellow schoolmate, Amber. And somehow, within the span of one single day, the teacher determined Katie to be the best-all-year-guide-and-friend to Amber.

Fast forward with me to the following summer where we worked a month long assignment at Young Life's Windy Gap. On day two Kathie runs to me in a bit of panic. She grabbed my hand and led me to a hidden view where we watched our now-ten-year-old playing volleyball in a wheel chair… with disabled teenagers. Laughing like never before.

Today, she works as a Teaching Assistant with special-needs high schoolers in Knoxville. She makes very little money, but she is leading incarnationally. Feeding, cleaning, laughing, asking, pushing, laughing, dressing, looking, laughing, hugging, crying and laughing. Katie is living their difficult lives with them… not just by caretaking but by seeking to know them. She is honest with them about them and honest with them about her. It is a beautiful thing to see.

Is this simply a sweet story that I can wrap up and bury in my soul? Yes. And a good one at that! BUT could it also disrupt my way of viewing how I lead others? Do I have a vision for me as I sit in circles to "lead" others along The Way? Can I have coffee with another while living a unique openness about who I am as "leader"?

I think I can… with God, in Christ and by His power within.

To the King,
BuddyO

#57

Dear Men,

My definition of Incarnational Leadership:

"Once upon an eternal time, God wrapped skin around Himself to bring us to Himself. And now He has done it again… but this time he didn't wrap, He entered. Within you and I is the very same Holy Divinity that can, like Jesus, bring us to Himself."

A few weeks ago I posed a question to a circle of about eight friends, all of whom are vocational pastors. "Would you rather be kind or aware that you are not kind?" The question was a bit of a jolt, and it took a few minutes to sink in. After some discussion, the room split equally: 4-4 was the vote. Personally I fell on the side of "aware that I'm not."

But as I have soaked in my definition of Incarnational Leadership, a deep sadness has risen within me because I am not a very tender person. Kindness is not a long suit of mine and it is bringing me some substantial grief. To relate and lead and love as Jesus does, a Fatherly compassion must be present. To correct and remind and disciple as Jesus does, a Fatherly compassion must STILL be present.

Of late I am missing that compassion. I have forgotten the love of my Father.

Yet what is very clear to me about me is this… I want to be tender. I want to be like Him in the ways of loving-kindness. I want to be patient with myself and with others as He walks with us on The Way. However faint, hope rises even in the midst of my grief that within me is the very same Holy Divinity that can, like Jesus, bring us to Himself.

Peace to you,
BuddyO

#58

Dear Men,

Several encounters have left me sad this past week. Upon review, the sadness has risen from my observation of men withholding themselves. You and I have not only witnessed this, but have also regularly participated.

It is out of fear of being wrong that I pull back from confrontation.
It is out of fear of being seen as too opinionated that I don't offer my two cents worth.
It is out of fear of "having to go there" that I don't go there.
It is out of fear of lacking grace that restrains me from being more incarnational.
It is out of fear of being misunderstood that I let another's foolishness slide.
It is out of fear of looking dumb that I refrain from offering a thought from left field.
It is out of fear that it's not my place, so I gossip about it instead.

I am super-fascinated how our culture (especially our Christian culture) lifts knowledge to the highest of all pinnacles. We think that understanding, education, and the intellect will lead us to the promised land of Godly living. If we can just walk RIGHT paths and make CORRECT decisions, then we can maneuver through each of life's difficulties (whether relationally, politically or circumstantially) to peace.

But in the name of RIGHT-ness, our faith gets high jacked. *Being Personally at Peace* is lifted to idolatry status. Our beliefs become secondary. And worst of all our Body-of-Christ-Family is seen as something to figure out instead of kinfolk who need to reminded of the love of God.

The common thread is obvious... we are more run by fear than openness to God.

Please don't misunderstand. I am not submitting that we cease reading the scriptures and studying the ways of God. But the ways of Jesus that we dig into will reveal a Man living out His love-for-the-Father with COURAGE. Perfect love for another is always laced with courage! Fear-based living (as described in the second paragraph) has self-love at the center.

Allow Paul to unpack this sentence – Perfect love for another is laced with courage!

I'm not writing all this as a neighborhood scold just to make you feel rotten. I'm writing as a father to you, my children. I love you and want you to grow up well, not spoiled. There are a lot of people around who can't wait to tell you what you've done wrong, but there aren't many fathers willing to take the time and effort to help you grow up.

I know there are some among you who are so full of themselves they never listen to anyone, let alone me. They don't think I'll ever show up in person. But I'll be there sooner than you think, God willing, and then we'll see if they're full of anything but hot air. God's Way is not a matter of mere talk; it's an empowered life. (1 Corinthians 4, The Message)

Wow, what courage! What love!

Paul sees that fear cannot necessarily be trained away nor can good advice cause fear to flee every time. Courage is needed... especially courage with God as we pray for discernment, understanding and the capacity to take the time and effort to help another grow up.

Any of you out there want to help me grow up?
It'll take the courage that you already possess.

To the King,
BuddyO

#59

Dear Men,

Imagine having coffee with me right now, for there are three things I want you to hear. Last night I had a dream, I told a story in the dream and I woke up with Scripture on my mind.

I.

Here is what happened in my dream last night. I was sitting at a registration desk in a church foyer... a big church foyer with a lot of men present. There was a bustling of good. Men of all ages (boys too) all glad to see one another. Some were gathered around me, some signed their name to a single sheet of paper sitting on the table in front of me, some of us exchanged stories, but all were busy occupying themselves with one another. It was a happening place. AND it was 9pm!

I had never seen so many men so alive in (what I consider to be) so late at night! I had been there all day enjoying the company of men and had decided it was time to go home. As I left I encountered two close friends... two of you. I hugged one while the other busied himself to enter another crowded and lively room which was anxious for him to begin leading/teaching his Spiritual Formation class.

(Sidebar – I am so proud of this man. In this present day he is giving his thoughts, time, care, hours, heart and life toward the hopeful formation of souls here in Knoxville and beyond. He says yes to SO MANY things that I would turn down. As a result, he is invited to places I am never invited to go because of his tenderness and openness to God. I am so honored that he would call me a friend.)

Everyone was enthusiastically staying late into the night with one another in hopes of growing in their faith. My friend was about to begin leading their discussion. And I was buttoning up my coat to leave. End of dream.

II.

In the exchange of stories (during the dream) I told this true story to a circle of men: "When I was eleven, one year after my dad died, my pee wee football coach had this conversation about me with my mom:"

- Mrs. Odom, would you please take your son off the football team?
- (Startled) Coach Fox! Why would I? Is he doing something wrong?
- No, Mrs. Odom. He's a great kid. He's just not good.
- He doesn't do anything well?
- Well, yes… one thing. He helps guys off the pile.

This is an actual encounter that my mom had when I was a kid. And no, she never took me off the team.

III.

Immediately after waking, this scripture from Revelation 20 came to mind:

Then I saw "a new heaven and a new earth," for the first heaven and the first earth had passed away, and there was no longer any sea. I saw the Holy City, the new Jerusalem, coming down out of heaven from God, prepared as a bride beautifully dressed for her husband. And I heard a loud voice from the throne saying, "Look! God's dwelling place is now among the people, and he will dwell with them. They will be his people, and God himself will be with them and be their God. 'He will wipe every tear from their eyes. There will be no more death' or mourning or crying or pain, for the old order of things has passed away."
He who was seated on the throne said, "I am making everything new!" Then he said, "Write this down, for these words are trustworthy and true."
He said to me: "It is done."

I am quite aware that the words <u>It is done</u> are the exact ones He uttered from the cross.

Gentlemen, it is finished. We live <u>in</u> the present but <u>from</u> the future. What I am saying is this: Button up your jacket and go! Whether you help others off the pile or walk slowly with others as they discover new ways of interior formation, go! Whether you are restoring a brother gently to his faith or getting to know a new friend, go! Don't wait on another to come to you... for the One already has. Go! Live out of the reality of the new heaven and new earth. He is with us now and in a (somehow) more complete way then.

Trust His done-ness with your worry over your friends. Trust His done-ness with your marriage. Trust His done-ness with your vocation. Trust His done-ness with your health. Trust His done-ness for your children. Trust His done-ness with your future... because the old order IS NOT THERE!

There, all things are new.

To the King,
BuddyO

#60

Dear Men,

I am not sure what I will write in #61. And I DO hope I am around to write it. But if I had one thing to say, one last letter to write you… it would contain these straight-as-an-arrow words from Annie Dillard:

"One of the few things I know about writing is this: spend it all, shoot it, play it, lose it, all, right away, every time. Do not hoard what seems good for a later place in the book, or for another book; give it, give it all, give it now. The impulse to save something good for a better place later is the signal to spend it now. Something more will arise for later, something better. These things fill from behind, from beneath, like well water. Similarly, the impulse to keep to yourself what you have learned is not only shameful, it is destructive. Anything you do not give freely and abundantly becomes lost to you. You open your safe and find ashes."

This is not about leaving a legacy. This is not about being transparent and authentic. This is not about my writing or Kathie's painting or your passion. This is not about discovering your dream. It's about something much, much deeper.

The honey that you and I have, that resides in our bones, that is meant to be squeezed out by our living is our love.

You know the love I speak of, for only the believer has it. It is the unadulterated and unshameful purity that all other love is only a shadow of. It is the Faultless that makes its way through our attempts. It is the Redeemed that converts our poor efforts. It is our unexplainable Three-in-One God Almighty that has virused us.

Spend it.

Waste not another moment… Make that call. Write those you have disappointed. Apologize to her. Make that list of men that you want to contact.

Shoot it.

Do not hesitate. Failing should be an assumption. Doing it poorly should be expected, not feared. But conversion by the Great One is the assurance, so

Play it.

While you and I have longings to love and relate better (which are from God), there is no need to cower because we have a history of disappointing others or a deficiency in being able to articulate love.

Give it, give it all.

When I am waiting for my attitude to improve or that deep forgiveness-that-even-forgets to show before moving toward another, then I am not moving with the Energy of the Holy Spirit. Instead, I am snuffing out the possibilities for the infection of love to spread. Even though affection may not flow naturally... when I do not hold my children to my chest and voice their beauty back to them with custom words, then I do not reflect the nature of the Father. When I see a potential misstep of a brother and refuse to lovingly inquire because I am the chief of sinners and have no right, then I do not see the love of Jesus in the Gospels with clarity.

Lose it, Men.

Leave it on the floor. My ability to forgive may come later. Feeling may come too. Anger and judgement might dissipate right before your eyes. But if you and I are waiting on a certain arbitrary level of Godly behavior or character before exercising the Holy-Spirit-saturated-love-of-God-residing-within, then we all suffer.

Give it now.

To the King,
BuddyO

#61

Dear Men,

I've been looking forward to processing this ache with you. It's been with me for such a long time, like a muscle cramp that tries to tell me: You're doing something wrong.

Each of us have spent a lifetime being evaluated… either in social settings or institutional. Take a moment to reflect on the impact an every-six-weeks grade card (for at least twelve years) can make on a child. It is a loudspeaker of sorts barking You are a failure, You are mediocre or You are above average.

Yet one could easily see the advantages of how personal score-keeping pushes, raising the bar to encourage another to fall in love with learning. I love to read and write now because someone(s) pushed me to more. And I thank them.

As a thirty-something-year-old I remember one book in particular that awakened my senses to God like no other. Brother Lawrence's *Practicing the Presence of God* slowed my life. This classic aided me to become increasingly alert to an ever-present God who was actively loving me during the crazy years of marriage and child rearing. But it also touched the now formed scorekeeper within me. My seasoned paradigm was this – receive all input (read a book), decide if I approve of the input (grade it), create an openness to the parts I favor and reject those parts I don't.

In regards to Brother Lawrence's book, a personal dilemma arose: While I applauded, appreciated and even longed for his practice of companionship with God, I also began to ask myself… how does my practice compare with his? How often do I notice God with me? (Compared to Brother Lawrence, I give myself a D+). How long has it been since recognizing His nearness? How can I shorten those times in between? Why can't I seem to walk simply in His joy and be increasingly mindful instead of forgetful? My senses are not sharpening with age like Brother Lawrence, am I missing something here? What discipline can I engage to improve?

Cramp.

Again I awoke this morning grading my senses, and I simply don't like doing this. This desire for growing in love for God and others seems often to conflict with how I sense I am advancing in this love. Does Unending Grace have a secret eye in the sky? Or is it possible that I am operating from the wrong senses of my feelings?

Dallas Willard offers this: *What is running your life at any given moment is your soul. Not external circumstances, not your thoughts, not your intentions, not even your feelings, but your soul. The soul is that aspect of your whole being that correlates, integrates and enlivens everything going on in the various dimensions of the self. The soul is the life center of human beings.*

If I am to live in a truly alive sense – as I read any book or speak with any person or be confronted with any surprise – then I must live from my soul. Not through willpower or mental calculation or the influences of another or even how I feel. And (here's the best part) it is the soul that my God has saved... not just my heart or mind or body or relationships.

Soul-Sense engages all these other aspects of heart, mind, body and family into my living and loving. Soul-Sense offers peace even when my body fails or my mind can't scroll up a cure for loneliness. Soul-sense lets me read Brother Lawrence without feeling the pressure to compare. Soul-sense allows me infinite room to practice disciplines while living in freedom. Soul-sense is oblivious to earning, because the soul has been redeemed.

So smoke a cigar to the glory of God today. Toast the One who has bought your soul. Your soul can love that person that irks you, even though your mind and heart say otherwise... it makes Soul-Sense.
To the King,
BuddyO

#62

Dear Men,

What if my last act on earth
Just before my death was to be...

A looking back to see
Me from yesterday.
The one who took Sunday nap,
Walked the neighborhood,
Slept with his wife after
A meat loaf dinner.

And then behind him stood
Me whose gray hair was shorter than today.
But no one could tell or
Care for that matter as
I skipped my bath and packed
That box and emptied
That dishwasher.

The daily multitude of tasks and thoughts
Now forgotten because I slept (or tried to)
Fill the space
Between each me standing single file
More foolish and more handsome
As the line of youngers snake upridge.

As I step slow each set of eyes connect
With mine...
An aging Backwards.
The memories no longer familiar
As stories but returning,
Accumulating like deposits not to be
Forgotten, swelling me with light.

Though 20,000 Buddy's stand in wait of re-introduction

I walk deliberately,
Feeling my hips swing,
My neck turned. They are to my left
Why I do not know.
But it is all I do not know
Now seeing these

Stronger men and
New dads eager for friendship,
Sabbaths and laughter.
They care less and care
More.

Tighter skin, corneas white like one
Who never swims or looks away,
These young men are restless,
Impatient to build and do.
Their love odd as mine today.
So too their passions.

And now here he stands straight
as a broom-in-corner.
The one before she came.
He was Fiction till today, a legend
To my kids.
We shake hands before I hip
Forward with twenty years of me
Before me.

I am amazed by him. Not the me
I meet but the one who is somehow
Containing himself in stride. Until the
Sixteen-ager shows, who in one blink,
Is gray, ashen.
A wanderer in search of Home.

For the first time, I reverse to
Lay eyes again on the redeemed me

But cannot.
All before me, though increasingly
Boyish, shorter and
Briefly acned,
Hold an isolation in their
Soul.

A hue which ever remains through
Baseball, broken arms and the
Funeral. The presence of (even) a good father
Yields no color.

I am smaller.
As are the days and the line and
Certainly cuter.
The boys corralled from play
Not wanting to stand
To see this old man.
Or sit in his lap.
Or lay in his arms.

But they must before the last come.
The first day, the last
Me.

What greets me afterwards is a
Fullness... a fan of others
Spreading deep and left
Deep and right.
Two Grandfathers different as
Corn and Las Vegas,
New Blood and old laying
Their skin and touch on my
Skin and touch. All
Moving into me and one another.
And the building light
Lifts me above to see the vastness of
It all.

Them all.
No more ash. No more gray.
All elevating me with their beaconing pride
Growing beneath.

And I rise
To the King.
BuddyO

#63

Dear Men,

I sit in the kitchen this early morning in an almost perfect silence. But for the hum of Freon moving through the refrigerator condenser coils and the morning waking from the short night with bird-speak, I can hear nothing.

My senses are keen to the quiet this morning because of last Friday's high privilege. I watched a friend die.

The beginning and end of life are equally miraculous. While happening to each human, nothing prepares us for the surprises in tow when witnessing birth or death. Only repetition can dull the senses (and then only somewhat)... like an Obstetrician working labor & delivery or the funeral home director.

But for folk like me who long for awakening, surprise is to be embraced.

As a matter of fact, I wrote a letter to you about some of the surprises that impacted me. The letter, according to my wife, was "as beautiful as you have ever written". Kathie continued, "But some things you should hold onto."

What immediately came to mind was a quote from a desert father named Diadochus of Photiki: *When the door of the steambath is continually left open, the heat inside rapidly escapes through it; likewise the soul, in its desire to say many things, dissipates its remembrance of God through the door of speech, even though everything it says may be good... Timely silence, then is precious, for it is nothing less than the mother of the wisest thoughts.*

You know me... I tend to live out loud (remember the Annie Dillard quote from #60?). I view discernment as something people hide behind, not fully giving themselves in relationship. But viewing discernment as a path to knowing God or as a way of quietly guarding the intimacy I have with Him or as a means of incubation for my spirit, well, that is a great kindness He offers.

Certainly there must be private ways that the Trinity has within Himself, relational styles that He has yet to reveal for He has discerned that I am not open/prepared/ready. This does not mean that God is holding out on me (which at times I secretly believe). Instead, we now have the mind of Christ AND complete access to the Throne of Grace (1 Corinthians 2, Hebrews 4) which allows us to know Him, not fully now but later. What a fun thought: God knows me so well that He has discerned what is best for me to see or not see… for my good and His glory.

Practiced Silence coupled with *spend it all-shoot it-play it-lose it-all-right away-every time* might be the greatest of all disciplines. I imagine confession to be this… creating an interior quietness which allows space for the emergence of forgotten/unknown/hidden sin so I may readily shoot it all/give it all back to the One who paid my debt.

You may pray for me to know this way of confession.

To the King,
BuddyO

#64

Dear Men,

I have a friend who lives in another country... one far, far away from here. One where you and I might naturally think: WHY on God's green earth would anyone CHOOSE to live there?!

He will probably return home someday in the not too distant future, but lives with deep consternation over moving back to a place that would elect Donald Trump as president, sleep-at-the-wheel of all things Godly or quietly champion a competitive environment between Christians (you know, catholic vs. protestant vs. left vs. right, etc.).

What would you say to a man who rightly sees America as a country in deep relational deficit? As he wonders, "Is there any good in the US?", how would you respond? What is alive in you when you begin to think on your own choice of sides, whether political, ideological or who you choose to spend time with?

This morning I was reading about how Moses kept a veil over his face to cover the fading glory. But today, we as Christians (whether we live in America or Brazil or Moscow) have nothing to cover up. Christ now meets us face-to-face. He has removed the veil and allows us (though not yet entirely) to live in His presence regardless of our political or cultural surroundings. More than allowing us, He energizes us with His Spirit to be awakened to the reality of His nearness! In that awakening we will know Him more and increasingly look like Him.

Light is needed where darkness persists and God is placing you and I on the edge of that very darkness, not to be tempted, but so the Light may penetrate. For instance, what do I say to the friend that enjoys watching The Bachelor? How do I intersect with an irritating neighbor now that he has moved out because his wife wants a divorce? How do I relate well with a dear friend who sees his own sister as out-to-get-him?

This country I live in is dark. No doubt about it.

The only good thing about darkness is that it allows for the light to be needed. Darkness gives a backdrop that allows your and my changing-into-the-likeness-of-Christ to stand out. Darkness cannot put out light, therefore, NOTHING can consume nor devastate us. Not foolish decisions, arrogance, job transfer, misunderstanding, the pain of loss or dreams that won't materialize.

While standing on the edge of darkness, no matter how you define it, remember this: God has relationally tethered us into Him, to (however dimly) reflect the reality of that teathering. My location may change by choice or providence, but that teathering cannot change. True darkness no longer exists because you are teathered.

To the King,
BuddyO

65

Dear Men,

When I am sick, I need medicine. When I need to know why my cholesterol is high, I need a blood test. But when I am dying, I need a friend.

Of late I am suffering from this recurring ailment I've had since birth known as Opinionation. It is rooted in the Christ-within-me that loves excellence and righteousness and the ways things were created to be in the First Days. But it travels through the house of sin located at 1111 Buddy Odom Boulevard.

Opinionation squeezes beauty from excellence so that I may have impact. Opinionation subtracts relating from righteousness by adding my version of the law. And Opinionation pollutes the order of the universe through my greed and demand to be necessary.

No surprise, but our culture helps zilch. Since our churches often live in ways that are linear, methodical and strategic, another strain emerges called Solicitation of Opinionation. Well-meaning but misguided friends help fan the ugly of my demise by gathering opinions for all directions in the name of equity. Once I am asked and I have responded, I am both less because I have spoken and fueled like a drunk man to drink again.

The most painful symptom of my illness is my inability to be still. My iPhone is not far away, I can no longer sit for substantial periods, my mind floats, I am easily distracted and, I am easily (so easily!) inclined to make judgments... of the personal bent.

Are there not succinct proverbs that might curb my endless desire to toss in my two-cents? Is wisdom not available to help whittle my *Incurvates in se*?

The answer is yes. But words, even scripture, are just an advil for the present crush upon me.

This friend I spoke of in the first paragraph is One who forgives. (Along with me can you hear this in your own personal judgments and opinions?) He is One who knows you and me thoroughly as His prize. And He promises to be actively and presently working out my salvation for my good and His glory... which gives me incredible hope. It is not the arrival of a healthy man (me no longer opinionated), but the hope of a sick man that is the fragrance of Christ to a fearful world.

While I am restless He is at work to love. In me and you.

And that's no opinion.

To the King,
BuddyO

#66

Dear Men,

To pick up where I left off last week: Opinion-givers (of which I am one) are not sinning because they are giving their input, thoughts or personally formed observations. Instead we sin when that offering is grounded in self.

Because of Kathie's career I spend time with several artists and have witnessed their extreme talent up close and personal. Many love to paint, want to paint, need to paint and, may I say... are called to paint. To follow this strong urging, "traps" that seem unavoidable lie ahead. Paint, canvases, brushes, mineral spirits, easels and frames are a great expense. To paint means to use these up which requires a replenishment which requires money which requires sales. Now the trap (temptation) is set. The opportunity comes to reduce prices, cut corners, with inferior product, allow someone to tell you what to paint or undercut another artist.

At this point it is good to remember that temptation is not a sin. Is it a sin for an alcoholic to walk into a bar? No, but it's not really a good idea. These "traps" do not reach out and catch my foot. But they are there ready to help me insert foot into mouth... usually by compromise to who I am in Christ.

Shmuel Yosef Agnon writes, *An author* (or painter, I might add) *who believes he has great things to write about himself misappropriates his mission. The individual to whom God gave an author's pen must write of the acts of God and His wonders with human beings.*

I find that my most common prayer is for sobriety of soul and the sobriety of self, and for an awareness of the trap of compromise which leads me to offering the unsolicited opinion. As I end I will pray for your sobriety too.

To the King,
BuddyO

#67

Dear Men,

I must admit that, when something bad happens to me, something that upsets my emotional or comfortable equilibrium, I do not respond with "What a privilege to share in the sufferings of my Jesus."

I DO, on the other hand, believe it... that personal hard times and trouble actually avail me the privilege of knowing Him with more realness than ever before. And with time my beliefs are coming around, be it ever so slowly.

I believe it because age offers nothing but downhill stuff. At this reading you may feel, as the Boy Scout Oath suggests, physically strong, mentally awake and morally straight. But a little more age demands that you and I confront our beliefs such as what I just mentioned above. My body is breaking. I can continue to ask why and look for the reasoning of God, or I can lean into the Person.

I love the way Peterson translates a piece of 2 Corinthians 4, *Our lives are at constant risk for Jesus' sake, which makes Jesus' life all the more evident in us. While we're going through the worst, you're getting in on the best!*

But what does this slowly-coming-around-living-into-my-belief-while-surely-being-at-constant-risk look like? And are there ways to cultivate a greater assurance that God is indeed winning all these battles of fear and doubt that are fought within me?

Two answers come to mind: Slow down. Be grateful.

While everything in my little world begs the opposite out of me, I am finding that time and beauty is the greatest mixed beverage.

In my little world I am actively pursuing some good relational living by planning, saving, being careful and arranging for good. Yet there are better things to consider when it comes to living my last days in love... being more still, writing a letter, reconsidering what I know of prayer, hoping for depth, wasting some time, enjoying art on my walls, thanking a friend and maybe even risking that very friendship.

As the plant fades and the flower dies, so does the faith in our bodies wilt... as it should be. But there are many things (mostly relational) that carry over. May we pick those up and walk over together,

To the King,
BuddyO

#68

Dear Men,

I love surprise. Remember the afternoon game show called Let's Make a Deal with Monty Hall? Do you want what's behind the curtain or what's in my pocket? How about $500 or what is in this box? And at the end of the program were three doors, with the promise of ONE of them hiding a new car! Who wouldn't like a good jolt like the ones Monty offered?!

Well, come to find out, her name is Kathie Odom.

I remember a moment in counseling with Kathie years ago when Roger (the counselor) told me, "You do know that Kathie hates surprise, don't you?" What?! How is that possible… it's un-American! It's un-Christmas-morning! It's un-motel-room-door-opening-to-find-fresh-beds-that-you-don't-have-to-make-before-leaving!

Not everyone likes surprise. Maybe I don't as much as I think I do.

Last week Kathie and I returned from being out of town for an extended period of time. During the drive home both she and I were bombarded by texts, messages and phone calls… we were heading directly into a cloud of hurt and pain in East Tennessee. We had just left my brother who had surgery near the brain stem and entered lives labeled by:

- My wife demanded that I move out by Friday.
- We've called in Hospice for my husband and the AC has been out for three weeks.
- My job is in under threat, the hospital bills are piling up beyond our ability to pay and I'm in a dark place.
- The most loving thing I can do for everyone is leave my wife of 27 years.
- I'm pulling out of a commitment to you and my small group.
- The doctors have done all they can for my mom.

In my surprise I whined (or maybe boasted) about all this over the phone with a friend who said the most perfect words that I was able to hear: Welcome Home.

I came home to my people. Not a job to do or something to fret over or situations that needed Superman or storms to weather or shrapnel to remove or fears to overcome or problems to fix.

You and I live in a place. This place of yours and mine have people. If you need to remind yourself of this somehow, then create a T-shirt that says WADE IN. In doing so, you will come home to them. And not be so surprised.

To the King,
BuddyO

#69

Dear Men,

Two things are colliding in me lately.

1) As of today I have now lived 21,846 days. Over 60% of these days I have been married and, on one hand, most have felt quite ordinary. Laundry, work, meals, shuttling kids to school, church on Sundays, fights, make-ups, vacations, daydreams and hopes, dodging bullets, blessings, financial decisions, holiday decisions, exercise, gray hair, setting the alarm, going to bed and waking up to do whatever it is all over again.

2) I want to live an increasingly robust-in-God life, fully-formed, wealthy in every way (this phrase borrowed from The Message, 2 Corinthians 9). I want to live this life (again, increasingly) in regards to the mundane (laundry, gray hair, etc.) and I also want to live this life when I am confronted with myself as I have been this week.

This week I held onto frustrations, a need to control, angers, perceptions of me, impatience, arrogance, desires for recognition (especially in small things and especially from my wife), my time/calendar. I have been a hold-out to others by keeping small accounts. And I've also kept an unrighteous, unholy distance from others by quietly demanding they live like me.

At this point, my temptation is to ask the question: As I retain all these things in different measure, how can I increasingly live a robust-in-God life?

But what if I rephrase this fair enough question? What if I began this question with WHO not HOW? Frankly, I'm not exactly sure how to do this, but I like the idea of beginning with a relational query instead of systematic (WWJD) one.

It is 24 hours since that last paragraph and a few things have happened since I posed the idea of asking a WHO question in regards to living a robust life in God. I am presently in Montana with two other wonderful couples, but barely know them. Kathie and I are spending most of our time with like gender... so I get to be with these two 60-something avid sportsmen and successful businessmen who are already friends with one another. In other words, I sit in the backseat a lot, literally and figuratively.

I find that I so want to be included. Wait, I can say it better than that... I don't want to be a joke to them. So I end up seeking ways to Champion Myself.

You don't do this, do you? You don't find yourself on the outside of a circle, both literally and figuratively, and then create ways to be seen, do you? You don't have any vocational leadership skills that subtly elevate your humility to your people, do you? You haven't spent any of your 21,846 days championing yourself because your wife won't for you, have you? You haven't compromised your character by morphing to be more like others than like God, have you?

Well, I have.

But I have also (am also) begun to ask more of a different sort of question. Not How can I get better? But more like Who am I? Who are these I get to be near? Who is this old friend like now, instead of How can I better understand the predicament he is in?

Thanks for taking my letters.

To the King,
BuddyO

#70

Dear Men,

I have exchanged several emails and enjoyed conversations this last week with many of you regarding #69 posted last Monday. One aroused something within me. Here is how it went…

Him: Buddy, your quote "desires for recognition (especially in small things and especially from my wife)" struck a chord in me… Amen to that! Here's to a robust Jesus-close-life!
Me: Yes! Hey man, can we think together over the next few months on: WHO not HOW? WHO is the person sitting across from me called Kathie (insert your wife's name here) Not: HOW can I get her to understand me? Or see me. Or love me. Or even trust me.
Him: Ummm… I like it… I'm in! Who is my sweet bride? A beloved daughter of the King!

As he said this about his wife, I realized how often I do the very same thing — I run to the truths of God (it's a great thing to believe that my wife is a beloved daughter of the King!) so that I may progressively live out of those beliefs. But here is my problem: I find that I often want to do this more than anything! As the example goes, I want (more than anything, which can also be translated: primarily) to believe that my wife is a beloved daughter of the King, and then live a life like I believe that.

There is _nothing_ wrong with that, EXCEPT when I make it _primary_ to knowing God. Listen carefully to this again in a different way — When I am seeking to live an increasingly robust-in-God life by having a belief system (having good and right answers to good and right questions) without knowing Him, then I am doing the HOW over the WHO.

Well, of course, Buddy, no one thinks that we can have a truly Godly life WITHOUT knowing Him!

Yes, but we live as though we can.

How often I have done a great thing (like my friend) by seeking a proper and correct answer to a question that will inform how I live. Who is Kathie? (This starts with a WHO, but note how seeking-an-answer quickly moves it to a HOW question). She is a beloved daughter of the King! (I have no contention with this answer, except that, while it nails the question, it changes very little in the same old ways in which I relate to her. VERY little transformation on my part!)

And why is there little change in me toward Kathie when I primarily seek to live out of my beliefs? Why do I still get my feelings hurt when I don't seem to be on her radar screen or when I don't understand why she doesn't want to snuggle? It's because I am looking for an answer so I could move onto HOW I can respond. I am seeking to live an increasingly robust-life-in-God without knowing Him first.

A robust-life-in-God can happen when all my beliefs start to crumble beneath my feet. When God seems absent. When my wife is pissed at me. When money runs out. When my body fails. When people don't understand me. When I am depressed.

Primarily, people are not meant to be solved, my life is not a big question to be answered and relationships are not meant to be navigated. These are, on the other hand, wonderful things to be enjoyed.

WHO questions invite us into both enjoyment and knowing God. HOW questions (even masked ones like WHO is my wife?) try to solve life's dilemmas.

So, I ask you, wouldn't it be good to sit and wonder over your wife? Wow, who really is this woman that I know so very little about? Wouldn't it be lovely to simply enjoy her (yes, this beloved daughter of the King) without quietly wishing she would stop talking so much or spending so much or drinking so much or arguing so much or worrying so much? Wouldn't it be good to just marvel more and say yes more?

Maybe I can get there by asking Who while not looking for an answer. Maybe I can have beliefs that develop while not using these beliefs as a means to make-my-life-better. Maybe I can seek to enjoy while not demanding that my life be navigated smoothly. Maybe I can let all the people in my life come to me without condition. Maybe I can know Him regardless of how on target (or off target) my beliefs are.

The Spirit of God has made me for such good purposes.

To the King,
BuddyO

#71

Dear Men,

Before I had this receding hairline I made a public spectacle of myself long ago.

I took my twenty-three-year-old self and pompously displayed my foolishness by marrying Kathie Hearn. Foolish because I had no idea what I was in for... Pompous because I was going to be the best husband on God's green earth.

Why is there not a law to keep the young Buddy Odom's from doing this? If you have to be sixteen to pull onto the interstate, why should you not be required to wait until at least thirty before pulling a woman into your adolescence? During the Christian ceremony, why didn't someone stand and say, "We all know this guy... there's not a snowball's chance that he will breathe life into this beautiful young woman! Somebody stop this madness!"

One of the beauties of God is this: You and I are embraced as we are not as we ought to be. There is somehow no prerequisite such as courage, brilliance, grit, wealth, affection, fortitude or heart to come to Him. As a matter of fact, **foolishness** might be our greatest accessory as we move forward in learning to relate as God relates. For if we were to know the future well, there is no logic available to help us overcome the fear of it all.

I have stood before God and made promises to Him.
I have stood before Kathie and made promises to her.
I am a fool.
And all of this works together because...

In both my faith and in my marriage I have been carried.
In both my faith and in my marriage I am being carried.
In both my faith and in my marriage I will be carried.

This doesn't mean I will cease to be the fool. Nor does it mean that God will cease being the One who loves me and carries me into the unknown storms ahead... and into the glory of His Kingdom that I can only glimpse this day.

Happy 36th anniversary to us!

To the King,
BuddyO

#72

Dear Men,

The king of our land is a subtle, penetrating and dominating presence in the lives of everyone I know. He spreads his existence like a virus and all embrace what he offers. I continually bump into this self-proclaimed monarchy of souls, this silent and intoxicating siren who hypnotizes each and every one of us into justifying our allegiance to him. Those who claim Christ as King may be the greatest of fools and I, as one, turn my allegiance all too often to this throne-stealer.

I would like to make a formal introduction. You will enjoy gazing upon his tanned appearance, Sinatra-voice and all-inclusive laid back approach to all things self-centered. May I introduce you to – The king of Ease.

king Ease hails from everywhere for he originates from within the flesh of us all. His life goal is to, at all costs, give you and I more for less. More property for less money, more life for less exertion, more freedom without commitment, more health at less cost, more happiness with less effort, more credit for less work, more advancement with less engagement, more revelation with less inquiry, a greater reputation with less integrity, a stronger marriage with less conversation and deeper relationships with less investment.

Maybe the greatest power this king enjoys is his ability to lull us into a trance. Before I know it, I live entitled to more-than-what-I-presently-have and quietly demanding that God supply all-good-things-that-I-don't-presently-have. If my wife is not loving and caring, then shouldn't God awaken her? If I don't have a husband, shouldn't God give me one? If we are childless, why would He not allow us a pregnancy?

With a loving wife my life would be EASier, with a husband it would be EASier to not look so unwanted and it would be EASier for my spouse and I to understand our future with a child to raise up.

Dear Men, notice how inclined we are to worship this king of ease. Notice how often we are pained by the difficulties of life... whether it is picking up your kids' damn toys for the forty-eleventh time or the inconveniences of growing old.

The True King promises no life of ease. What He (Christ the King) does promise is:

I will give you all you need to increasingly know Me more.
I will not leave you.
I will hide you in Me.
I will live in you.
You will do even greater things than I have done.
You are my child.
I will go to the Father on your behalf.
I will give you my heart.
You will never ever live a life apart from Me.
I belong to you.
And you belong to Me.

To the True King,
BuddyO

#73

Dear Men,

I hope this letter is a more than a little FYI. It is meant that you might know me a bit more AND consider reading a good book... you know, one that comes highly recommended to you from a friend.

I have long had a shelf that contains my Top Ten books... my absolute favorites. If you look close, you will count eleven because it's a bit preposterous of me to keep a good book out of the Top Ten. BUT when I read one that knocks my socks off enough to make it in, I won't add (to make it twelve) I will replace one of the eleven. Just how my twisted-self works sometimes.

There are three books by Wendell Berry, one memoir, two fiction, one biography, two art books, and a straight-up book of sermons. They were penned by a couple of Brits, a couple of Catholics, a translator, a couple of Presbyterians, a Quaker and I wish there was more than one woman.

Here are eleven VERY brief rundowns, one on each book.

The Return of the Prodigal Son by Henri J.M. Nouwen. There is a deep reverence reflected in the way this book is crafted and bound. The high gloss photos and fold-out details of Rembrandt's masterpiece, coupled with Nouwen's Luke 15 reflections, are just the bones to a slow feast. It is unfair to call this a good-read, it is more like a slow long bath. It's a must to buy the hardcover first-edition and buy as-new-a-copy-as-you-can-find!

Harlan Hubbard by Wendell Berry. This is a biography of simplicity whose name is Harlan Hubbard, born 1900. He and his wife Anna lived in Payne Hollow, Kentucky when not afloat somewhere on the Ohio River. If you are inclined to read out loud to your wife before bed, this is your night cap.

Jayber Crow by Wendell Berry. Lee Scruggs gave me this book upon its first printing in 2000 and it has been, and forevermore will be, my favorite novel. It's about the life of a barber and I have read it maybe ten times.

Fully Alive by Larry Crabb. The way Crabb goes about unfolding a biblical understanding of gender and how we relate one to another is jaw-dropping. When he translated the Greek word for female, I cried with joy and couldn't wait to find words about my own masculinity. Crabb begins with a quote from Irenaeus, "The glory of God is a human being made fully alive" and builds from there. You may not know it, but you want to read this book.

The Pastor by Eugene Peterson. The life of a pastor is the most bizarre existence I can think of. To walk with others in their messes, to spend an uncommon amount of time in prayer and to set yourself up for failures on a grand scale is standard operating procedure. I have spent a lot of time with a lot of pastors and if you read Peterson's memoir, you will understand why I love them... in their beauty and in their foolishness.

The Gaze of Love by Sister Wendy Beckett. Open the book to any page and you will find one painting or sculpture opposite one reflection by Beckett. This is an exercise for the imagination to swim in God. I cannot speak enough about this little book but words water it down. My requirement for you upon acquiring this gem? Limit to only one page/day.

Godric by Frederick Buechner. Not for the light-hearted or lazy reader... the loosely fictional Godric (God's-wreck) will challenge the harshest spiritual critic (one like me who thinks my theology is most closely aligned with God's theology). This one will wake up your slumbering soul.

The Great Physician by G. Campbell Morgan. If I could buy a book for everyone I know, it would be this book of sermons. And the subject of Morgan's sermons is simply Jesus. Several times I stopped breathing when he spoke to me of my Master and His way with others. Every book falls short of a relationship with a friend, but Morgan helped me see and know Jesus like nothing I've ever read before.

The Strangest Way by Robert Barron. Over the next couple months four friends are joining me to read this contemporary work of walking the Christian path. Chapters entitled Finding the Center, Knowing You're a Sinner and Realizing Your Life Is Not about You does not make for a best seller. But it DOES make for courageous disciple.

A Timbered Choir by Wendell Berry. Each Sunday Wendell goes for a walk with pencil and note pad resulting in what he calls his Sabbath poems. I am reminded why I enjoy the writings of this man when I pick up this collection... his hands are dirty.

A Testament of Devotion by Thomas Kelly. Skip the first 30 pages as they are devoted to remembering Kelly. When I jumped into the first of five short chapters I immediately discovered a new language for God and a new illumination of God that shapes me even till this day. I skimmed all the good of Quaker-ness without having to wear suspenders or live in Pennsylvania.

Happy reading To the King,
BuddyO

#74

Dear Men,

As stated in my last letter I have joined four friends in reading one of my Top Ten (or eleven) books, The Strangest Way by Robert Baron. Immediately Baron seizes me again with beautiful articulation…

"Deep down many of us Christians still believe that God is a rivalrous Lord who dispenses favors grudgingly, only after a demonstration of virtue on our part. (But) the true God is not one who loves in a niggardly or calculating way, but one who IS nothing but love, not one who offers Himself as a reward, but one who gives Himself away as a gift."

I believe this, I see this, I preach this and even champion these words. Therein lies my personal difficulties. Statements like these from profoundly dedicated-to-God believers can easily become a platform for me. (Do you see this in your own interior world?) I feel myself "amen-ing" as I read words like Baron's which at best can only add another plank to my already girded belief system… that is, if I simply keep reading.

Why do I say this? Certainly I could proceed with unpacking the right-ness of his sentences to you, but that feels a bit empty. What seems proper (with these awakening words before me) is to stop and ask, how do I see this belief manifested in my life? If what he says hits so soundly within, then there must be a present reality in my own life that aroused me… so, what is it?

This was not (and is not) an easy task, at least I did not find it easy for me. But may I offer three ways I have seen myself demonstrate virtue so that God may dispense favor toward me?

- When I haven't prayed for a while or haven't recognized His presence with me or haven't exuded gratitude back to God, I find myself approaching Him with a touch more formality:

"You do not deserve to be treated with such absence on my part, Lord. Because I come now, would You see and hear and consider my request to know You more deeply?" (Good prayer, but sent to a possibly unwilling God).

- When I go to my PO Box to see what $ may have come in for Echo Resources, I can feel my prayer life amp up a bit. Not like days of old when I was anxious and called on the Lord of the Harvest to fill my account, I now use my I-trust-You-to-give-as-much-as-You-give-when-and-if-You-give to remind Him that I do actually trust Him. (Good virtue, but sent to a God who needs awakening).

- When I think about how to spend my Sunday mornings (church services invite the worst out of me), I consider how to re-say my church-pains to God, because He has not revealed much hope to me. "There must be the perfect phrase You could utter through a friend God, to help me find an ounce or two of joy when I walk into a worship service." Since He is mostly silent on the subject with me, I am prone to think there must be love He is withholding until I get all this figured out, so I employ my how-long-oh-Lord-how-long-must-I-wait angle. (Good night, what a bad theology!)

May I caution us when we read something we like or find ourselves agreeing with a political pundit. Even though it's a bit of a thrill to find someone who shares our beliefs, may I encourage you to ask, why is this good thing so good to me? Why is this thought of God so invigorating?

If we stay for a bit, we might find ourselves opening up to the love of God who comes as a gift.

To the King,
BuddyO

#75

Dear Men,

As this email is being sent through the internet and to your device, I am somewhere over the Atlantic coming home. Kathie and I had never been to Europe so we seized the chance for her to take an oil painting workshop in the Northern Italian town of Lezzano on Lake Como (known as the residence for George Clooney). We went early to Venice and stayed late for Florence and, I am sure, will come home changed.

Kathie and I are known in many ways by many people. Not only does much of our world revolve around her active painting career, but we are avid art enthusiasts as well. Translation: We are art lovers. We research artists, collect original pieces, visit galleries wherever we go, buy books on art, talk it and marvel at it. We don't have pictures or stuff hanging on our walls, we have paintings. If we were loaded, we'd have more of them.

The crown to our trip, the one thing I would again pay all this money for, was to experience an exhibit by Bosnian artist, Safet Zec. Giant pieces of tempera-painted on newspaper and canvas that hung from the rafters depicting the agony of a war-torn people.

One piece shook me to the core.

Over the alter of an ancient church that housed the exhibit, a ten-by-seven-foot masterwork seemed to drip tears onto every brave soul willing to sit beneath it. Two men were being lowered into the arms of others. No faces, just arms, ribs and rope. I could almost smell the pain of loss as the living assisted the dead to descend. My own death felt so near as I was lowered alongside my Savior.

There are so many directions our reverent-imagination can take us when we use meditation and art. The thread that took me to the deepest cavern of exploration was when I noticed the title of this piece: Hanging Body.

Body? There were two!
Until I discover how shallow I define the word "Body".

Those of us in Christ are ONE with Christ.

To the King,
BuddyO

#76

Dear Men,

I would not be entirely honest if I did not share with you the goodness it is for me to write these weekly letters. It causes me to stop and consider… consider before God and you what is stirring within me. I believe that is a distinct way of praying for me.

And isn't praying a process? How many prayers have I uttered that were also simple acts of me just having a conversation with a friend or night-dreaming something absurd or going for a quiet walk or laying sick in the bed or looking out the window ala The Twilight Zone? I remember mowing the yard once and rehearsing a never-before-happened argument with a friend (that I won, of course). This had happened countless times before while in the lawn with the same guy (again, all this was within me) and I, all of a sudden, grew very tired of these accumulated bitchings… so tired that I said aloud, "My Lord, would you <u>please</u> take ALL my past and present grumblings and turn them into prayers for this friend who irritates me?"

An immediate response came… Of course! my Lord said to me.

Could it be that you and I try two things that might seem to oppose one another? 1) Take it easy on yourself when it comes to failing at strategic, intentional, planned prayer. See your life as a living/walking/fretting/hopeful/forgetful prayer and offer grace to both yourself and others when it comes to our views on prayer. 2) Set aside time to sit still in God. Knowing that prayer is already occurring within the Godhead ABOUT you, sit in Him with your life's concerns and hopes. Yes, Jesus and the Father are talking with each other about you, even as we speak, and you can plan time to listen in. It takes calendar chunks and a great imagination (which He has already given you), but I will assure you that putting the cell phone away and doing this will mean a substantial increase in your awareness of His love.

Or write. Journal. Speak. Ask someone what their name is. Move toward irritating people. Say a long hello to your neighbor. Think about what gifts to give to others. Linger. Whittle. Compose a song or a letter.

All may just be prayer.

To the King,
BuddyO

#77

Dear Men,

I was a young buck once, thinking forward into the future... wondering of things like:

Would I marry? No was my assumption.
Pastor a church, maybe? Never.
Stay in Tennessee? Of course.
Have a farm? I sure hoped so!
And how old would old be?

I landed on a number rather quickly, because I changed the question to: How old can I NOT imagine myself to be? I've never forgotten that moment back in nineteen-eighty-something and have revisited it quite often as the chosen number approached. Fifty. Even as a young dad, I could never imagine myself being fifty years old.

Yesterday I turned sixty.

I sit in a quiet room this morning <u>trying</u> (trying is the operative word here) <u>trying</u> to reflect on it all. What I am tempted to do is google charts about the life expectancy of the American White Male. But that is not reflection, that is fear.

Thanks in advance for the well-wishes, but would you stop and consider this... Like me, do you move toward fearful action when offered a quiet opportunity? Last week I had a surprise moment that forced me to slow down with a new perspective. For a couple hours nothing mattered but gratitude to God for the life He has given me and the people whom He has given to me.

But soon, in the middle of this wonderful moment, I found myself looking for company... you know, someone to share it with. Treasuring it up in my heart for too long seemed selfish. But in actuality it was the fear of being alone with God that made me pick up the phone.

As much as I have known of loneliness, I have spent sixty years trying to escape it. It's kind of like fasting with me; I have learned to stop eating for 20 days, but I have yet to treasure it. I may have become friends with silence and solitude, but have also found a way around them by hosting retreats and not participating. At this age I can get away with more because I am much more practiced at deception than your average bear.

Yet lately I am beginning to see that fearful action is less and less of an option because quiet opportunity is increasingly being forced upon me. Young fellas are asking fewer questions. Couples are seeking less input. And few are the ones who line up to pay the real live cost to belong solely to God.

I get it.

The cost of confronting fear and sin and foolishness and past and intentions and doing-the-things-i-don't-want-to-do and stupidity and embarrassments and ... well, it feels easier to let the Larry Crabbs of this world do it and let me just read the book.

Thanks for this birthday present, this day-after to reflect on sixty instead of run from it. I certainly don't want another sixty years BUT I absolutely want to hang around to watch my fearful actions decrease. And I really do want to treasure others more deeply... ones like you.

To the King,
BuddyO

#78

Dear Men,

I have written this letter now four times. The first three times I tried hard to address my greatest interior enemy, Entitlement. All that I wrote was worth sending to you, but I simply couldn't put meaningful enough words to what I really wanted to communicate.

So I'm going to put it straight. I can't, you can't, find any life in holding onto your demands. And these demands-to-live-life-like-I-think-life-ought-to-be-lived are oh so subtle and oh so insidious.

Insidious – (in-**sid**-ee-uh s) – 1) intended to entrap or beguile, 2) stealthily treacherous or deceitful, 3) operating or proceeding in an inconspicuous or seemingly harmless way but actually with grave effect.

We do not know and are not aware of how destructive our entitlement spirits are. We end up…

- Separating ourselves from people we love.
- Judging others without full understanding.
- Feeling like we have full understanding when it's not possible to have it.
- Justifying our anger.
- Encouraging others to follow our anger.
- Avoiding conversations with those who are angry with us.
- Spiraling downward while flipping off our true Family.

All because I demand that I am right.
And demand that I cannot be wrong.
And that there is no way in heaven or hell that you can tell me differently.

My friends, when I stop long enough to consider the preposterousness of my smallness in the light of the Great One, I might be humbled. And the grave effect of my demanding-ness shrinks a bit.

Would you stop for a moment and consider (with me) how thick your entitlement armor is? Whether someone has pulled into your lane or pulled into your private space or pulled into your soul. Please. Let them. Give them room that you don't want to give. Give them a humble nod. A quiet opening. A quiet invitation to come on in. And watch for God.

To the King,
BuddyO

#79

Dear Men,

I wrote last time about entitlement and ended with these words...

Would you stop for a moment and consider (with me) how thick your entitlement armor is? Whether someone has pulled into your lane or pulled into your private space or pulled into your soul. Please. Let them. Give them room that you don't want to give. Give them a humble nod. A quiet opening. A quiet invitation to come on in. And watch for God.

An old Young Life kid of mine borrowed a word or two from this paragraph and, after reading #78, shot a simple text back to me saying, Thanks for giving me some room.

Looking back to those days, I must confess how difficult it is for me to imagine giving <u>anyone</u> some room, especially at the age of twenty! But I know this guy well (he was in my wedding and we are current still today) and I know he wouldn't lie just to make me feel good. This text came from a deep place within him, so I must believe that what he is saying is true!

Go with me as I break this down a bit to see why this is true.

Let's start with a big statement that may seem insignificant at first consideration: <u>In the Garden Adam and Eve were hungry</u>. God created them (all of us) with thirst, desire and longing... of course for Him. But after Adam took the first forbidden bite, his hunger got misdirected and twisted (we call it sin). But notice – the hunger never left!

You and I hunger. That is GOOD news! And this hunger is the foundation for both my 1) entitled spirit and 2) His redemptive work on the cross.

<u>My Entitled Spirit</u>

I hunger, therefore I turn to things to fill me. Oftentimes these things are classified as good or bad, but ALL are idols when my spirit turns expectantly toward them to satisfy this beautiful hunger. But expectancy can quickly turn to entitlement.

Take for example, when someone obviously and purposefully pulls their car into your lane. A variety of angers emerge out of you at this point. Why? Because the law of the land has deemed that *that* space belongs to you until you leave it or yield it. It is yours. If someone drives their car into your car while it is stationary (in your space that you are legally given) then they are liable for the injury to your car and your person. Your rights are violated and you have legal recourse.

Within me, like a mile-high stack of pancakes, are what I have deemed to be the rights of Buddy Odom, aka my entitlements. I am predisposed (see "sin" above) to law not grace. And I protect my rights given by law (what's right and what's wrong) because these rights are mine and you can't pull into my lane or shame my daughter or disrespect my opinion or have my time without permission or fail to be there for me or say that I am entitled. I have rights!

Actually no. I don't have any rights. But I do hunger.

When you and I see someone fall or speak with foolishness or commit adultery or pull into your lane, may God help us see this person's hunger before seeing his failure.

You see, I showed up in my friends' life when he was in high school and I quite naturally screwed up. I'm sure that I fell, spoke immaturity to him, had an affair with being a Young Life leader (got my rocks off on the attention), and cut him off from being more of him because of my insecurities, BUT...

Jesus' Redemptive Work on the Cross

took into account my hunger and my friend's hunger. And God also took over all my sin and my friend's sin on the cross.

One of my favorite daydreams is this: Imagine words coming out of your mouth. And in super-slow-motion, while the words are suspended in the air before your friend hears them, God changes them into what He wants them to be. From one hungry man to another... Conversion in the air!

This is one of the redemptive works of the cross that happens all the time. And it happened regularly with my high school friend back in the late '70s. That is why he wrote this truth to me – "Thanks for giving me some room."

In my hunger and through the gracious work on the cross, I <u>did</u> give him room. And you know what else? It was reciprocal. My high school friend fed my hunger with friendship... and we started growing up together.

Letting another pull into your lane is a good thing... for him and you. And me!

To the King,
BuddyO

#80

Dear Men,

If you've read the last few letters, then you must love me deeply OR the words have struck a chord within you. Either way, keep reading because I got more.

It doesn't take an award-winning therapist (do they pass out awards for excellent counseling?) to see that my writings of late are more about the journey God has me on instead of an insight I've been given. This entitled spirit thing, this compulsive demand I have to be important, thought of, seen, considered or invited-to-the-table is gradually being revealed to me... about me.

As I lay in bed this morning in some kind of prayer with God, I was able, somehow, to see several of my insecurities. After waiting through it I began to see that these insecurities are the basis of all my petty angers and prince-like entitlements. Are you like me in this? Can you see the trail of your low-level grumblings (especially relational) and trace it back to the false need to matter? Read this question again with me... Can you see the trail of your low-level grumblings (especially relational) and trace it back to the false need to matter? And can you see how it is all based on a thick sense of insecurity?

But, the greater my security in Him is, the stronger my sureness (faith?), and the less need I have to depend on another to come through for me, which leads NOT to anger but to forgiveness and a friendship that has no strings attached.

And, in Trinitarian relating, we can actually do it. Not perfectly or all the time, but it IS possible!

I have a friend who has left the reservation, as the old saying goes. He has decided to abandon relationships in spades, ignore all truth-tellers, throw in the towel on anyone and everyone who does not agree with him, spread ill-will and relate as though nothing has changed. He has given me and others plenty of excuses to give up, plenty of sin to point out and plenty of opportunity to pray for him.

But something profound hit me. I miss him. And when I recognize my sense of loss and sadness, a Trinitarian way of relating surfaces. So I texted him those three words that are the most truthful thing ABOUT ME. Instead of focusing on his vacating the premises, I turned my attention to ME and the loss that is most alive in me. When I wrote, "I miss you", I began to discover a forgiveness within me that I've never experienced before, a forgiveness that seems to trump all foolishness and injury and a forgiveness that smells like Jesus… the One who came back to say Shalom to His disciples-who-left-the-reservation during the time Jesus needed them most.

Forgiveness cannot come from insecurities, wounded-ness, finger-wagging, I-told-you-so's, comparison, or my understanding of truth. It comes from looking upon the love the Father has for the Son and the love Son has for the Spirit and the love the Spirit has for the Son and the love the Son has for the Father and the love the Spirit has for the Father.

When I begin to <u>supernaturally</u> (that's the key word) realize that I do not need another to bolster my ego and give me confidence, then I can increasingly go in larger measures of security in Christ to love. Ugly angers and petty-living start to evaporate, a new and righteous manner of forgiving sneaks in my back door and (brace yourself for this) your love starts to stick out like an unwanted addition to your kickball team. Yep. This sort of all-embracing love that pierces all armors will be a beautiful thorn in the side of your closest people.

Because our closest people also long for this… to actively love like Jesus loves.

To the King,
BuddyO

#81

Dear Men,

In ways incalculable sin crouches at our door. Seemingly harmless and even inviting to our desire to bring hope and healing into chaos, the opportunity to fall is ever-near. Oddly our cry for justice (may those who hurt others be brought to right and when I injure another, may I carry the burden of guilt) intensifies our anger not our love.

With so much absence of love in Christians like me, what am I to do? With the realization that the literal heaviness of my entitlement armor has caused me to become an invalid, who am I to be?

Who is the strongest person on the middle school basketball court when Lebron James checks into the game? If a healthy JJ Watt lines up across from you on the playing field, who in the entire stadium could stand against his power?

I'll tell you who... the referee. The one who oversees rightness and equity according to the ways laid out for all who walk onto the court. The one who enforces the boundaries on his field. The one who has the whistle.

If it is true that being the smartest, strongest or most experienced Christian cannot completely shed me from the sin of my demanding-spirit then, with so much absence of love in Christians like me, what am I to do? With the realization that the literal heaviness of my entitlement armor has caused me to become an invalid, who am I to be?

Three Beliefs followed by One Practice.

<u>#1 - The Supernatural (not the Natural) is in charge</u>
This is the reason why I do not call these Four Practices instead of Three Beliefs and One Practice. Developing my life with disciplines

(a Disciple is an apprentice "disciplining" himself/herself in the ways of the master) is me pointing my naturally-inward-turned-self toward the super-nature of Jesus. But, by these practices of forming my spirit, I cannot rid myself of the entitlement armor that I carry... which would be solving a natural problem with natural solutions. My sin(s) are supernatural problems that require supernatural solutions. In other words, I cannot save myself!

But He can. May God soak me in Belief #1.

#2 - The Trinity Carries You
Keep a cool head. Stay alert. The Devil is poised to pounce, and would like nothing better than to catch you napping. Keep your guard up. You're not the only ones plunged into these hard times. It's the same with Christians all over the world. So keep a firm grip on the faith. The suffering won't last forever. It won't be long before this generous God who has great plans for us in Christ—eternal and glorious plans they are!—will have you put together and on your feet for good. He gets the last word; yes, He does. 1 Peter 5:8-9, The Message

So akin to Belief #1 is this – you and I are being carried.

I love how Peter couples the disciplines with God in this New Testament passage. To me he is saying "Remember. But when you forget, God has you in your forgetfulness."

Gather others around yourself that remind you of Godly things that you've forgotten. Read letters from people you love. Belly up to the table of the Holy Scripture. Enact disciplines, that in and of themselves do not carry you, but instead create fertile ground for a good memory-jog. Remember things that you already know. Remember Who has the whistle.

May God soak me in Belief #2.

#3 - Living Must Include Confession

To me there is no greater-discipline-lesser-practiced than confession... saying I am a fool to God and others, specifically recalling my folly, stating what is not so obvious to others but is to me and God, facing the sin in me that thinks I don't sin a lot.

Romans 12 reminds us: *Do not think more highly of yourself than you ought, but with sober judgement.* Confession helps keep the drunkenness at bay. But I want it to be more than something I DO in life... I want to believe that I cannot live without it.

May God soak me in Belief #3.

Practice the Dead Man

My son is a large man. 6'3" and 300+lbs. And he swears that he can take anybody to the ground (which, of course, challenges the high school's strongest left tackle and smartest champion wrestler). But Will wins every time. Every single time.

By practicing the Dead Man.

The two begin by locking in a wrestling grip followed by Will exercising his elementary moves on this teenaged mass of muscles. As the younger grows in confidence and secures a firm hold, Will suddenly allows his bulk to go 100% limp... and to the floor they both go. (sorry, I cannot help but chuckle with the vision this creates in my mind). His weight + gravity = youthful humility.

The Dead Man means to let go of self.

Practicing this (especially when it comes to shedding some of the entitlement stuff) will make you feel/look less confident, more naïve, less trustworthy, more exposed, less reliant, more uncertain, less impactful, more lightweight.

Wanting to be a heavyweight is what got me in the mess I'm in... thinking I can take others to the ground with my Christianambition, Christian-virtue and Christian-reasoning. But I was made to be strong in the ways of humility, surrender and love.

May God grant you and I courage to practice the Dead Man.

To the King,
BuddyO

#82
Dear Men,

And then there is gratitude.

We practice the Dead Man
Because we live the Live Man.
A month has passed since six decades.
While yet only
One Day it seems
Has slipped around me like a
Pick-Pocket.
If aware I would have shouted out
Take my days and enjoy for

There is gratitude.

What will the boy
Do with those days anyhow...
What would I have done
With the field strewn of used hours and
Moments?
It is forward we all move, rolling the dice
Crossing yet again
Tennessee Avenue,
Marvin Gardens and somehow
Slipping past the corner where
Justice is served.
I make it to Boardwalk only
To do again

With an aging gladness.

My trusty steed carries me well.
Past the thimble
And terrier to
The lipstick reds and

Emerald grass avenues.
Cantering toward the
Day when loop-ing ceases
And Endless is all there is.

Endless.
The circle will actually be broken
By and by
The leaves will turn and fall
No more.

Live the Live Man
The lad turns to
Shout.

Live the Live man
By and by.

To the King,
BuddyO

#83

Dear Men,

If you are younger than me, by ten years or more, this might be a difficult read. It could be a letter that hints to you of things you've heard about, but are not as inclined experientially to receive. Therefore, you may need these words even more than your elders.

It is about our bodies.

Let's start with some facts (as I see them) and then, allow me please, to make a few comments.

You and I have been given one body... no more, no less. This body of mine has been both neglected and delighted by myself. I have at times given it ecstatic pleasure and I have also exposed it to deadly viral elements (sometimes unwittingly, sometimes carelessly). With the exception of the curious and mysterious union of one, the joining of flesh to Kathie, it is the one and only body given to me. There is no other body for me to live into. There is no other body for me to live out of.

We reside within our bodies for a certain number of days, and this number is not determined by us. I will not be here to directly influence my great-great-great grandchildren... there is absolutely no possibility of that. While they will have their own body, one that will exist and operate much like mine today, they will never touch or overlap with mine.

In a giant sense, I age within myself... with my thoughts, hopes, passions, loves, fears, failures, expectancies, frustrations and dreams, all of which dull with time. But "within myself" there is so much more. There is a highway lined with others who cannot be complete without me. But even more so, we are connected intricately as nerves, a system that affects and is affected one to another. My years of neglect and years of delight shape the entire body, each of those given to me, but my body is who I have been given. In an even giant-er way, there is no "within".

The aging failures of my body are not a result of lack-of-attention more than they are a movement toward <u>another body</u>. Soon I will receive one that is both new and (somehow) familiar. While today I grieve others with a well-practiced absenteeism, there will soon be a day when my new body is wholly and perfectly another's body.

Today you may be living with a secretive low-level disappointment of yourself... I know I do. But if I were to see myself as a vital part of the whole, I might age well into this new-body-in-store-for-me. If I were to have a greater vision of myself on the highway, I might stop my car more often and get out, and greet those of my body with invitation and love. For my aging is not mine alone.

To the King,
BuddyO

#84

Dear Men,

Some sort of congratulations should be offered to you today... you made it through another Thanksgiving without killing anyone!

Most (maybe all) of us are acquainted with this fleeting possibility. Though smiles are cast abroad the turkey and cranberry laden table, we end up keeping our distance from some folk for a variety of excuses.

Uncle Hank gives me little more than a nod or a "You keepin' busy?"
Aunt Lily doesn't know me any more than what my mom spins to her.
Cousin Jake doesn't get me, or even seem to want to.
Cousin Janice is disappointed in her husband.
Andrew brings his new girlfriend.
My wife reverts back to some of her childhood ways.
And I grab another biscuit and occupy myself with the kids.

Because I am the oddest of ducks and can't stay in any conversation with my extended family for longer than 15 seconds (usually about the successor of Butch Jones), I implement one of my many gifts like hiding behind words or sulking-over-this-annual-requirement-with-people-I-didn't-select or retreating into silence or engaging like a seven year old. But MOSTLY I simply omit Buddy Odom.

I justify this vacating-the-premises-way-of-relating by <u>blaming them</u>. It's sort of like a political debate on CNN that goes like this:

- Uncle Hank says (or doesn't say) one thing to me.
- I internalize everything said as a shrewd attack on me.
- I process his statement with mach-speed internal speech (well, he must've heard from his wife, who heard from my mom, that a lot of my work is over a cup of coffee with other men and, since he worked 45 years punching a clock

as a machinist, he is now poking fun at my work by saying "You keepin' busy?")
- I filter out my do-you-want-to-trade-jobs-you-old-bore?
- Then, instead of wondering about him and what his world is like and how hungry he really is, I blame him for his lack of engagement or his pitiful life.
- Lastly, I play by his rules and give him an out by saying… yeah, pretty busy.

Look men, here are the two things I want to say…

1) Who is going to see Uncle Hank if not you? Who in your family has the mind of Christ for Aunt Lily if not you? Who has the heart for those made in the image of God (like cousins Jake and Janice) if not you?

2) You and I have another chance. Yes, Thanksgiving is only the beginning of the Ten Percent… those days between Thanksgiving and New Year's Day that occupy ten percent of our calendar. We have plenty of chances to practice relating like God does to folks we would never choose.

If you don't have an Advent book to read for this upcoming season, don't sweat it. Use that reading time and simply take the love of God that you DO know. And give it!

To the King,
BuddyO

#85

Dear Men,

See a man's actions and you know what he believes. Know what he believes and you will hear his words testify.

I am glad to admit that Kathie and I enjoy watching *The Voice* and *American Idol*. The raw talent some of these kids have makes me shake my head in wonder. We also love the small vignettes created by the show that are based on the longing for a better life that every contestant has… a hunger which they call their dream.

"Singing is my dream!" they say in tears of hope. But each time I hear this, I wince in sadness. I think to myself… yes, you are hungry, but there is only One true dream. And it ain't your voice.

Thinking that an achievement of ANY goal or hope or dream will bring me what I most long for (perfect happiness) is fatal. Or put bluntly, the pursuit of our dreams is deadly.

Here is why – we end up living a life of disappointment.

I see it everywhere. The gratitude for life-didn't-turn-out-the-way-I-had-envisioned-it is rarely found (except in a few octogenarians). Yes, disappointment is real and true and it happens in me, but I give it a pulse by quietly believing that there is some-thing, some-one or some-life that will bring me an unrivaled satiation and satisfaction.

I opened with this line: <u>See a man's actions and you know what he believes. Know what he believes and you will hear his words testify</u>. While words like "I am disappointed" may not be used, our lives testify to the way in which we are in hot pursuit toward a better life that must be out there somewhere.

My wife is a successful artist and is seen as one living out her dream. But she would deny it. Yes, she certainly loves both the hard work and the reward, but her words point to something very different. She would say something like: *My dream is to open myself to God. When I drop all my ideas of a better life and unzip my life to Him, a new and almost unperceivable bump comes, ever so gently nudging me in ways I am designed to go.*

And gratitude follows.

To the King,
BuddyO

#86

Dear Men,

The words we use always point to something deeper within. We all have people with whom we work, walk, worship and wait…. and, when I listen well, I can visit a deeper place where their truer self camps out.

Last week I wrote about a word that is used often in our conversations: Disappointment. The spirit of Disappointment (much less the word) has no place in the life of a Christ-ian. Of course I feel it's presence from time to time but it has no reality, no life, no pulse.

I am accumulating a list of words that have no place in my life. When giving great attention, you and I will notice how often these words (again, more importantly, the SPIRIT of these words) are used by one another. They have no place in my life because I am on the Way.

Last week Disappointment. This week, Navigate.

In our kitchen, over by the Keurig, we have a tiny little sign that reads, **The River is calling and I must go**. While you can swim in a river, sit by it, take photos of it, fish in it, listen to it, wade in it, skip rocks on it, bathe in it or paint it… you cannot navigate it. You may **think** you can, but you are simply moving from side to side as it carries you somewhere.

This river flows through all your day and the events within your day. Your appointments (don't navigate them), your finances (don't navigate them), those bad surprises (don't navigate them), the ways you relate (don't navigate them), the bent to avoid those who irritate you (don't navigate them).

Navigation (controlling your arrival point) in a river is a fantasy. It is neither yours nor mine to choose. Have you ever driven to

Townsend, got in an overinflated inner tube at The Y and floated the Little River with friends? This is what life in Christ is much more like – you and I are being carried by The River.

No longer do you have to get your ducks in a row before a hard conversation or gather ammo for a confrontation or weigh out your chances or ignore Uncle Hank or prepare for worst-case-scenario or fret over your inabilities to lead well, or educate yourself in proper procedures with specific sorts of people. You and I are being carried into these places by The River.

The River is meant for all those things I mentioned earlier (swim it, sit by it, listen to it, etc.) because The River is primarily meant to be enjoyed. For the River is a Person. The River is a He. The River carries you. The River is calling and you I must go. Don't navigate Him, just get wet.

To the King,
BuddyO

#87

Dear Men,

As a reminder I am doing a little series on "words I don't like". Or better said, words-that-express-a-spirit-that-I-have-but-don't-want-to-have. Two weeks ago I wrote about *disappointment* (or any version of the word... disappointed, disappoint, etc.) and last week I shared a few thoughts about *navigation*. Next Monday will be Christmas Day and I will write a letter to you about the spirit I hate the most and am trying (by God) to kick out the door so that there might be more room for Him.

But today? Drumroll please.......
Tricky.
Didn't see that one coming, did you?

Tricky is the cousin to *Navigation*. *Tricky* is the posture I too often take as I walk the Path, because I think that the Path (my journey of faith with the Triune God) has ways (tricks) that must be learned or I will fail to know God or see God. It is an attitude of legalism and carries with it a demeanor of arrogance.

Granted, you won't hear the word too often. But look closely at the angle many authors and preachers take as they 1) spell out the problem, 2) offer a solution and 3) suggest a difficult way to step into the solution. Nothing wrong to this point UNTIL there comes a suggestion that taking the step into the solution is complex or obscure or tricky.

Remember the River? You and I are being carried by the River over many hills and valleys. There is nothing complex to learn and no secret handshake to grasp. So when you hear the spirit of, "Now here's the trick" to having insight into prayer or doing church right or sharing the gospel with your neighbor or understanding a piece of scripture... then remember these things:

- There is now no longer any condemnation for those who are in Christ Jesus.
- God has made Himself known to us though Christ Jesus.
- He has torn the veil in two because of Christ Jesus.
- And we have the mind of Christ Jesus.

One night Kathie and I were sitting with a dozen friends in our living room (have I told you this story before? If I have, then no apologies… it's a story worth repeating!) We were having a wonderful and rare moment of drinking in the sort of truths that I just bullet-pointed above. It was a beautifully weighty few minutes together as the Gospel became palatable in the room.

Kathie had some clarity and declared, "I need to hear these things every single day of my life!"

The room and everyone in it gave a hushed nod. It was a strong and profound statement. To regularly swim in the truths that my-access-to-God-is-now-like-Jesus'-access-to-God is a life-stimulating way to be! We all wanted to shout YES… all but me.

I detected a little trickiness. Kathie was not demanding, she just wanted to know God with a deeper consistency. But without knowing, she spoke a tricky spirit… "If I can get this remembering thing down I can live a better life" was the quiet sentiment.

So I said, "No, you don't need to hear those things every day. It would be <u>good</u> to hear them, but you don't <u>need</u> to hear them for their truthfulness to remain."

Men, there is a power in realizing that I don't have to know the gospel completely… the gospel is about me being known. There is power in not having to hold on so tight. There is power in chuckling at my failing memory. I do not have to understand or navigate or get it right. There are no tricks.

To the King,
BuddyO

#88

Dear Men,

Make Room.
As your capacities decrease and your worries increase. Make Room.
As your memory lapses and your uncertainty remains. Make Room.

As your discipline wains, your impact softens, your name fades, your faith disappoints, your failures glow and your plans for tomorrow are on hold. Make Room for Him.

When the only thing you can grip are your love-handles, when your ten-year plan includes breathing and when the kids only need you for childcare, Make Room.

I know... you thought you would fret less. You thought the urge for comfort would pass. And you thought experience would equip you for surprise. You thought friends would stop offering solutions and you would start to love them more. You thought fears would subside. And while you still believe God-in-Jesus to be the answer, the number of questions seem to be on the rise. Like – *How do I make room?*

On this Christmas Day or even New Year's Day or tax day or another freakin' birthday or a random Thursday in June – How do I make room for the God-in-Jesus to be the God-in-me?

It is a big question that, I believe, God hears. But it doesn't seem to grab His attention like His other concern... He wants you and I to trust that He has already made room for us within Himself. He has made room for your spouse too. And your children. And their children. Because He embraced all of you and me on the cross, even our sin, He has room for our disappointments and judgements and fears.

He has Room. Let's step inside together to the King,
BuddyO

#89

Dear Men,

This past year Kathie and I have done a fair amount of painting and writing. Often we have pushed our chairs back, reviewed our respective attempts and given our craft a mediocre nod…. in a sense saying, good enough. She framed hers and I pressed *send*.

Every now-and-again it just so happens that, as Kathie likes to say, that one painted itself. I personally know that sentiment also. Letter #60 I wrote to you a few months ago was a work that I need to read or myself each day.

Your and my days are filled with flaws. And we know this to be true because evidence of our corrective efforts abounds. We want to be appreciated. We want to say it well. We want to have impact. We want to bring beauty. We want to (in a wonderful way) be like God. So we work work work to (here it comes) get it right. And the floor it littered with our failures, our flaws.

My prayer for you in this upcoming year, Dear Men, is…. Well, let me go ahead and pray it:

Dear King,
With an unflinching-Christ-in-us-sort-of-bravery, may my friends who receive this letter know they are being carried. It takes a massive amount of courage to release our demands while seeking to love, to let go of self and to rest in the journey you have for us. May they seek not to work work work to craft their lives, but may they point point point with the joy of the life You have given them. In the name of Your Son, Amen.

Men, you will have slam-dunk moments in 2018… it will be great! Moments when you might say, that one painted itself. But don't make an idol of that moment, just drink it in with a full and happy throat. Remember that you were simply pointing and He let you taste it. Then return to your day of being carried.

May this year not be so much about new beginnings that produced great fruit but may your 2018 be about pointing-with-your-life to the One and Only King.

To the King for 2018,
BuddyO

#90

Dear Men,

As I prepared for bed last night I acknowledged an anxiety within myself. I felt a peculiar response/prayer rising within myself, a quiet but sincere request… Give me a dream tonight.

I've done this only a handful of times in my adult life, but each time a powerful dream has been given. Knowing He would answer my request, my anxiety grew as I drifted into sleep.

It began in a campground we've never visited before. Kathie was settling in by unpacking the goods it takes to make a temporary home. At midday I decided to take a walk to the river. My desire was to walk/swim alone (I say walk/swim because I made my way downstream more like a salamander than a man, mostly on my belly). But there was to be no alone-ness. Two ATV's appeared, each carrying two unknown men and rambling in the shallow river in and out of my view (were they fishing?), sometimes quite near and at other times distant. We all promptly arrived into a very small (and insignificant) building, sort of a tiny laundromat, where I made a request of them… Do any of you have a ziplock for my iPhone? (it was in my pocket and I was fearful it would ruin).

No was their answer and I noticed how rapidly it was getting dark. I needed to get back. The scene shifted.

I am walking down a steep and winding hill as onto a woodsy farm. And yes, I am walking with others. My pace is one with meaning, head down with short and simple conversations with those who work their way into my vision. The trees thicken around and overhead while my head slowly lifts. The pace slows, a vague lightness illumines the space while the trail has now become a dead end cave, but NOT claustrophobic. There is a sense of arrival.

Twenty (or so) people, men and women that I know, are there. Some walked with me (including Kathie) and some were already at the destination. As I greet these friends with a kiss in this den, there is a sense of both loss and gladness. One young man (again, a friend) asks me to rest/take a seat and I decline, aware that my purpose has not yet been completed... to find bread.

After a short hunt, I find two end pieces (the heels of a bread loaf from the grocery). They are on a low shelf in the back of the cave, each individually wrapped in Saran wrap and nesting into one another.

Then I awoke.

How do you hold your dreams? As something to be explained? Or explored? Do you see them as insignificant? Have you ever asked God for one? Does that request carry a bit of silliness to you?

While books have been written and professions created to help others interpret their dreams (I'm talking about those we have in our sleep), for the most part we pay little attention to them. But for those dreams we create during our awake moments, those we have control over to logically shape to our likings, THOSE are the ones we end up investing our lives into.

I am not sure what to do with last night's adventure. It rings of past foolishness and a future hope, of embarrassment and invitation and of selfishness and forgiveness. But mostly of this: Walk in the light given.

To the King,
BuddyO

#91

Dear Men,

Recently I created a survey about "church" and invited several of my young friends (average age, 35) to take it. Twenty women along with twenty men replied and their responses have awakened so many things within me about this faith I have. After considerable reflection an already-known-to-me reality grows larger and larger….

I can get busy making my identity rather than receiving it from those things larger than myself.

I spent a lot of time on the construction of that sentence so it may bear repeating: *I can get busy making my identity rather than receiving it from those things larger than myself.*

An in-Christ-identity has been given to me, freely given! And I am invited to grow in the very knowledge of it. Yet, because I am easily threatened, fearful of what you think, preoccupied with appearance, motivated by guilt, sensitive to being exposed, guarded with my reputation and forgetful that God is doing infinitely more than I could ever hope or imagine within me, I spend a lot of energy constructing a Buddy Odom that has the abilitiy to both attack and protect.

But the presence of God in me continues to make this reinforced-ego-building-project of mine more and more difficult. He is intent on making me like His Son and He will succeed in His intention… with these four larger-than-me identity shapers that come to mind:

- Community – My often-hard-to-embrace people that I have been given.
- History – The Story of the Trinity with His people (which includes me).
- Earth – That square mile that I live upon.
- Mystery – His ways are SO not my ways, yet He carries me to them and through them.

These four (and I am sure there are more) identity shapers make me who I am. Better said, they invite me to receive who I am. They trans-form me (as I am open) much more than in-form. They are giants and do not shrink beneath my petty desires to shape myself in small ways; instead they are patiently heaven-bent on completing me.

At this writing I am having some relational tension with a good friend, a very good friend. He is one of my Community. It's the kind of tension that wakes you at 3:27am, as it did this morning, and stays too close throughout the day. As I tried to fall asleep last night I drove to his house in my mind's eye. In his driveway we stood (he on one side of the truck bed and me on the other) and had a conversation about the ways in which he was wrong. Note the following <u>subtle strategies</u> of both attack and protection I devise even in a daydream:

- I drove onto his turf hoping he would notice my courage to step into the mess and wishing him to see that I was braver than he. But in truth I was on the attack.
- The chasm of an empty truck bed kept us apart and I put it there.
- Conversation it was not. Lecture it was.

But Community is bigger than the quarrel. Community, not the arguments we construct and win in our own little heads, exposes a deeper sin than being right or wrong… it exposes our relational-sin. And Community invites me into knowing me-in-Christ.

Sitting in the story of how the Three-in-One Godhead relates to His people, opening myself to what/who is within one mile of my house, allowing myself to be carried by the One I trust less than I'd like to admit and giving myself in new ways to people I'd like to punch… as painful and confusing and wonderful as these will be, in the end, I will live more fully alive and others will see God.
To the King,
BuddyO

Notes on People I Referenced

#1 – Marc Hanson is a beef of an artist with a delicious oil painting touch and an even deeper soul than most know. You MUST follow him on Instagram or any path you can find! When doing so pay attention to his love of the land and how he honors it with his brush and palette. Few there are who quietly give a deeply rooted talent as he does.

#13 – Sister Wendy Beckett is widely known for her love of God and art (in that order). Get online and purchase *The Gaze of Love* immediately... you will not regret it.

#15 – Poetry cannot be underestimated. Do yourself another favor by subscribing to Garrison Keillor's *Writer's Almanac* for your inbox. Daily you will receive a marvelous poem and fascinating stories about authors. The German, Rainer Maria Rilke, is one man who has lyrically captured my imagination as he ponders the existence of God. We should all have a Rilke.

#23 – The author, A.W. Tozer, wrote with simple elegance and profundity. As a young Christian his books seemed like letters from a Godly grandfather inviting me to move from milk to meat.

#34 – The life of author and blogger Anne Lamott helps me stay sort of sane. In one sentence she can be as tender or as thuggish as I can. Her hunger is palatable. Her candor is refreshing. Her courage is comforting. And hope is her hallmark.

#35 – Many of us have a Lee Scruggs... a bigger than life man that makes you feel like you are the star of the show. Lee had a way of imparting serious vision with a jovial spirit. He was both abrasive and warm. And he had a touch with hand and language that I deeply miss these dozen years later... one that continues to shape the way I want to relate.

#38 – "just a guy" is the way Jim Branch characterizes himself. This guy is a dear friend to me and a quiet orchestrator of relational living. He spends his mornings praying in the Chick-fil-A parking lot and his days living with those who inhabit his one square mile in the state of Tennessee. His compilation and personal reflections can be found in the "Blue Book", a publication you will wear out once picked up.

#38 – Eugene Peterson rarely needs an introduction. But if there is anyone who has a more righteously critical mind of our present Christian culture… well, I want to meet him/her! I've read almost everything he has penned, but his memoir, *The Pastor*, is what you will order today.

#39 – Billy Collins. Always something fresh coming out of this great American poet.

#40 – Because of Wendell Berry my days of walking Papa's farm have not left me. Smells and cracking twigs beneath my feet sound of yesterday instead of fifty years, and I am reminded that the most observant and hungry creature walking this planet is a child. Wendell, you are the greatest man I have never known.

#60 – Please read anything Annie Dillard writes. Start with a few sentences from her website and you will experience a woman who knows who she is and who she should be.

#61 – As a young believer I had no idea that people like Brother Lawrence and Dallas Willard existed. Quite different from one another in their lifestyle and style of communicating, both timely marked me in my early days of growth in Christ.

#74 – Robert Baron .This Roman Catholic Bishop that uses Twitter is my kind of radical. He is not quite sixty and looks not quite thirty… but, wow, does he love Jesus!

Made in the USA
Lexington, KY
24 January 2018